D0515824

HOUGHTON MIFFLIN

Celebrate

INVITATIONS
TO LITERACY

Houghton Mifflin Company • Boston

Atlanta • Dallas • Geneva, Illinois • Palo Alto • Princeton

HOUGHTON MIFFLIN

Celebrate

Senior Authors

J. David Cooper
John J. Pikulski

Authors

Kathryn H. Au
Margarita Calderón
Jacqueline C. Comas
Marjorie Y. Lipson
J. Sabrina Mims
Susan E. Page
Sheila W. Valencia
MaryEllen Vogt

Consultants

Dolores Malcolm
Tina Saldivar
Shane Templeton

INVITATIONS TO LITERACY

Houghton Mifflin Company • Boston

Atlanta • Dallas • Geneva, Illinois • Palo Alto • Princeton

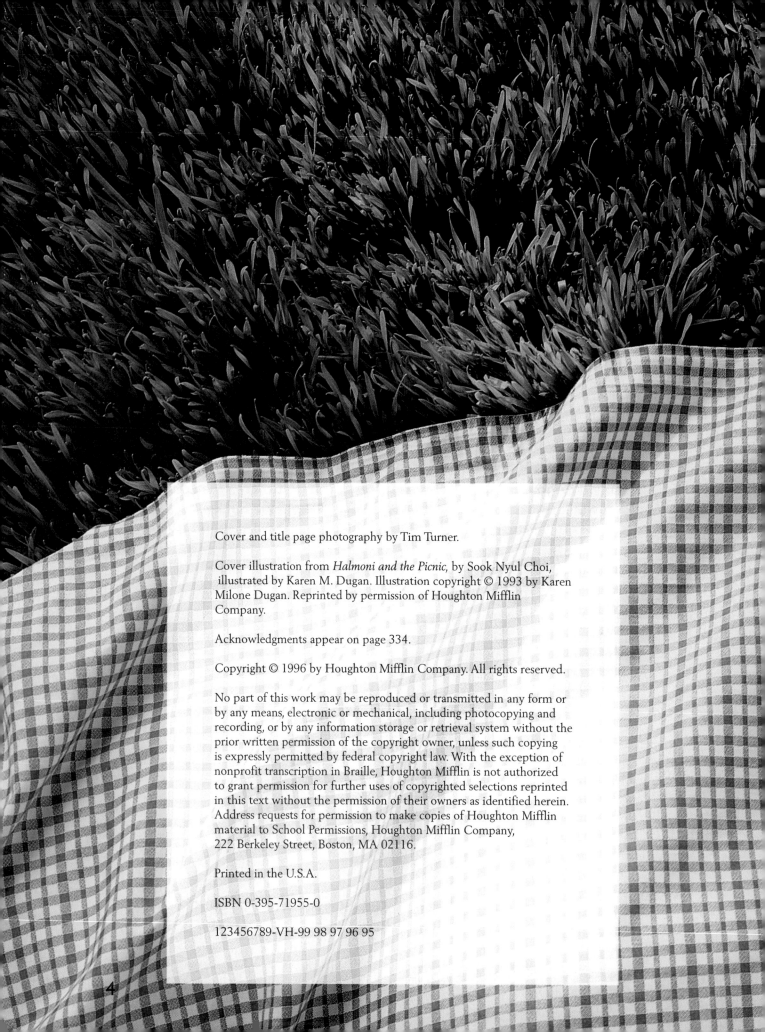

Cover and title page photography by Tim Turner.

Cover illustration from *Halmoni and the Picnic*, by Sook Nyul Choi, illustrated by Karen M. Dugan. Illustration copyright © 1993 by Karen Milone Dugan. Reprinted by permission of Houghton Mifflin Company.

Acknowledgments appear on page 334.

Copyright © 1996 by Houghton Mifflin Company. All rights reserved.

No part of this work may be reproduced or transmitted in any form or by any means, electronic or mechanical, including photocopying and recording, or by any information storage or retrieval system without the prior written permission of the copyright owner, unless such copying is expressly permitted by federal copyright law. With the exception of nonprofit transcription in Braille, Houghton Mifflin is not authorized to grant permission for further uses of copyrighted selections reprinted in this text without the permission of their owners as identified herein. Address requests for permission to make copies of Houghton Mifflin material to School Permissions, Houghton Mifflin Company, 222 Berkeley Street, Boston, MA 02116.

Printed in the U.S.A.

ISBN 0-395-71955-0

123456789-VH-99 98 97 96 95

Themes

CONTENTS

WHAT'S COOKING?

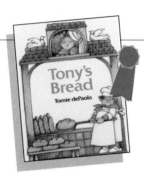

CONTENTS

Weather Watch

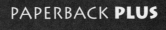
PAPERBACK **PLUS**

Kate Shelley and the
Midnight Express
historical fiction by
Margaret K. Wetterer

In the same book . . .
more about steam engines and
the real Kate Shelley

Yagua Days
fiction by
Cruz Martel

In the same book . . .
experiments and weather
facts

CONTENTS

PAPERBACK **PLUS**

····Contents····

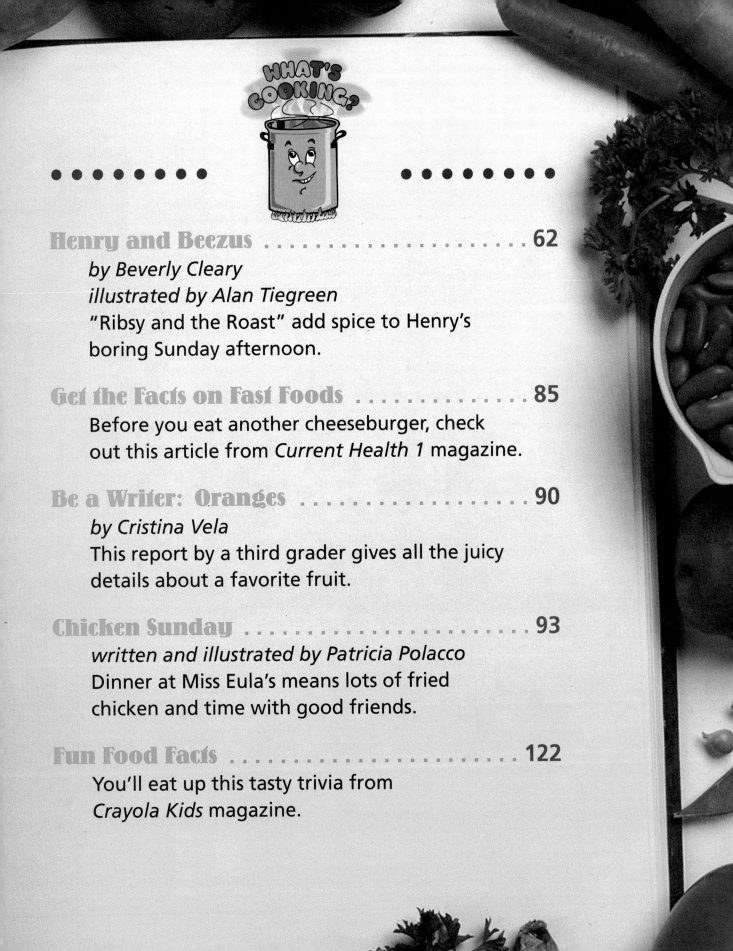

WHAT'S COOKING?

Who Put the Pepper in the Pot?

by Joanna Cole
Aunt Tootie's coming to dinner. With everyone secretly helping to spice up the stew, see what happens when Tootie takes her first bite!

In the same book . . .
Easy-to-make recipes and more fun with food.

WHO PUT THE PEPPER IN THE POT?

By Joanna Cole
Pictures by R.W. Alley

PAPERBACK **PLUS**

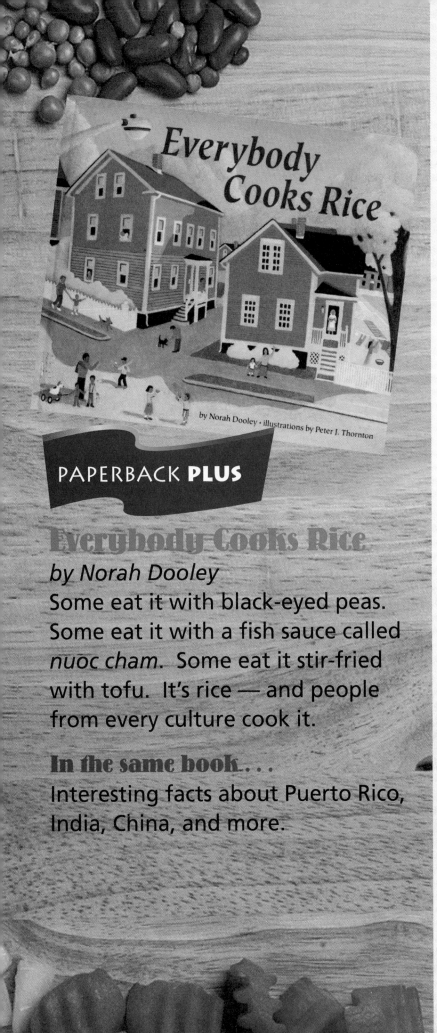

Everybody Cooks Rice

by *Norah Dooley*
Some eat it with black-eyed peas. Some eat it with a fish sauce called *nuoc cham*. Some eat it stir-fried with tofu. It's rice — and people from every culture cook it.

In the same book...
Interesting facts about Puerto Rico, India, China, and more.

Books to Nibble On

Aunt Flossie's Hats (and Crab Cakes Later)
by Elizabeth Fitzgerald Howard
A visit to Aunt Flossie's always includes telling stories and eating crab cakes.

How Pizza Came to Queens
by Dayal Kaur Khalsa
When Mrs. Pelligrino comes to New York from Italy, she brings a delicious new dish with her.

Carlos and the Squash Plant
by Jan Romero Stevens
What's that growing out of Carlos's ear? His mother warned him to wash there!

Siggy's Spaghetti Works
by Peggy Thomson
There's oodles of noodles and lots of pasta being made at Siggy's factory.

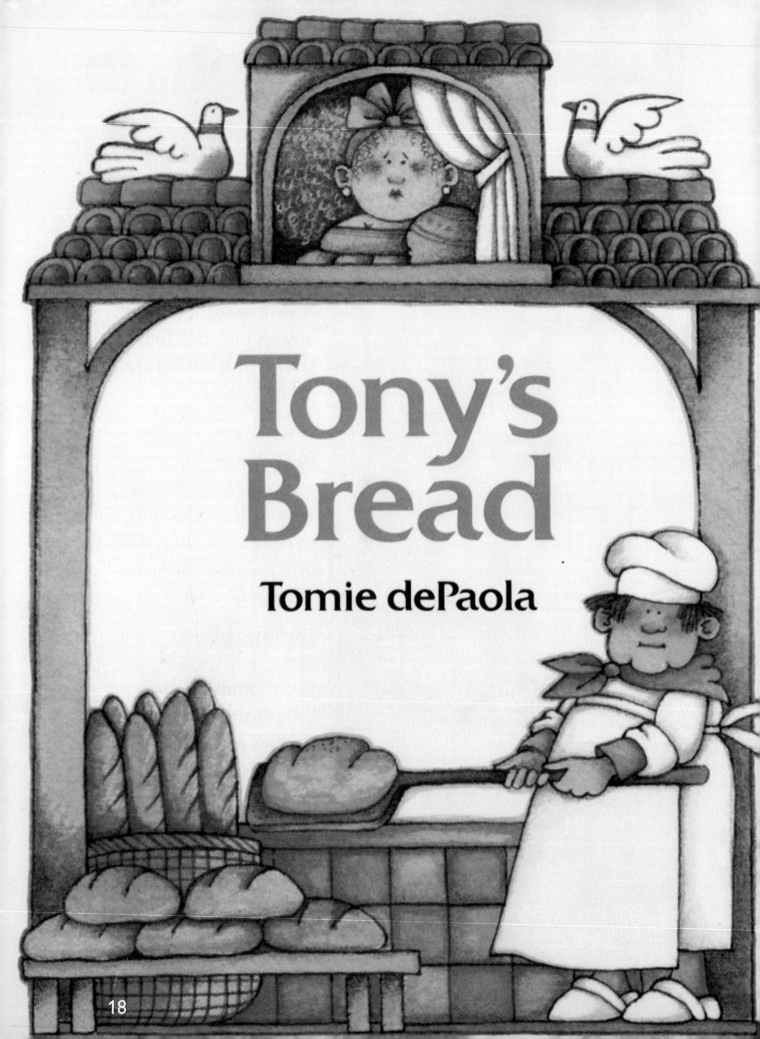

Tony's Bread

Tomie dePaola

Once, a long time ago, in a small village outside the grand city of Milano, there lived a baker named Antonio. But everyone called him Tony.

Tony made bread and only bread in his bakery. It was good and simple and the villagers loved it. But Tony had a dream. One day he would have a bakery of his own in Milano and become the most famous baker in all of northern Italy.

Now, Tony lived with his only daughter, Serafina. He was a widower and he had raised Serafina from the time she was *una piccola bambina* — a little girl. And how he had spoiled her!

"Antonio treats Serafina like *una principessa*" — a princess — said Zia Clotilda.

"The finest clothes, the finest jewelry, anything her heart desires," said Zia Caterina.

"She never has to lift a finger. All she does is sit, looking out the window eating *dolci*" — sweets — said Zia Clorinda.

"Now that she is old enough to marry, Tony thinks that no man is good enough for his Serafina," the three sisters whispered to each other.

That *was* true. Tony did think that no man was worthy of his darling daughter. He would not even talk to the young men in the village who wanted to court Serafina.

So, poor Serafina would sit at the window behind the curtains, eating her *dolci* and crying.

21

One day, Angelo, a wealthy nobleman from Milano, was passing through the village. As he went by Tony's house, the wind blew the curtains away from the window, and there sat Serafina. Angelo and Serafina looked into each other's eyes and it was love at first sight for both of them.

The three sisters were standing nearby. "Dear ladies," Angelo asked them, "who is that lovely creature sitting at that window? *Che bella donna!* — What a beautiful woman! Is she married or spoken for?"

"Ah, young *signore*," said Zia Clotilda. "That is Serafina, the daughter of Tony the baker. No, she is not married."

"And not likely to be for a long time," said Zia Caterina.

"No one is good enough for Tony's little Serafina," Zia Clorinda explained.

"Well, we'll see about that," said Angelo. "Now, aunties, tell me all you can about her."

The young nobleman and the three sisters sat and talked and talked and talked. And before long, Angelo knew all about Serafina and Tony the baker. And he knew all about Tony's dream of becoming the most famous baker in all of northern Italy.

"*Grazie*, aunties" — thank you — said Angelo. "I think I have a plan that will give Tony his dream and give me the wife of my dreams. But I will need your help. This is what I want you to do . . ."

The next day, a letter arrived at the bakery for Tony

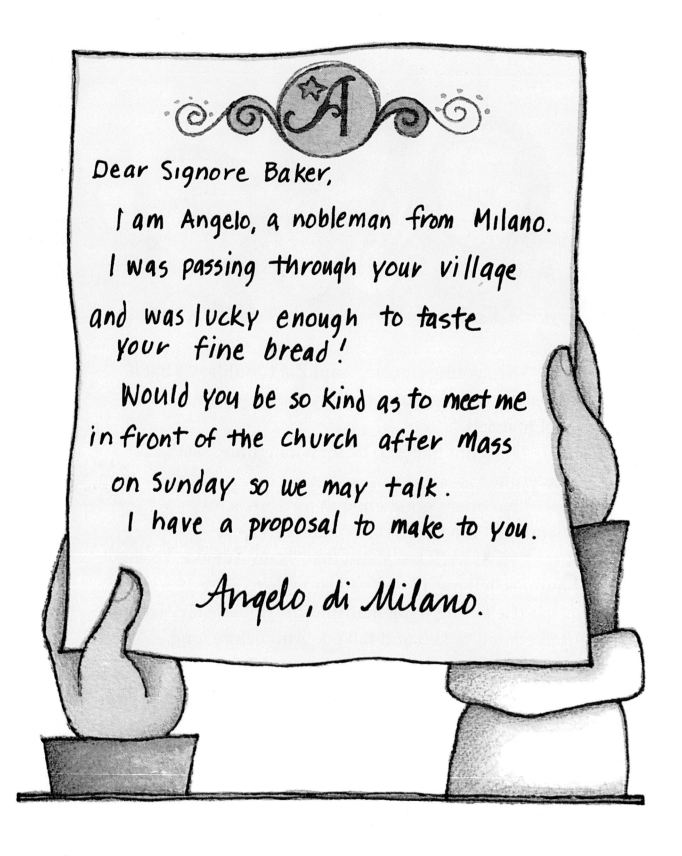

Dear Signore Baker,

I am Angelo, a nobleman from Milano.

I was passing through your village and was lucky enough to taste your fine bread!

Would you be so kind as to meet me in front of the church after Mass on Sunday so we may talk. I have a proposal to make to you.

Angelo, di Milano.

and a secret letter arrived at Tony's house for Serafina.

Dear Bella Serafina, ♡ ♡ ♡

I saw you at your window and I love you!

Here's a ring to keep as a symbol of my adoration.

It will not be long before we are HUSBAND and WIFE!

♡Angelo, your true love.

And Zia Clotilda, Zia Caterina and Zia Clorinda did their part.

"Oh, Tony, did you see that rich young man from Milano?" Zia Clotilda asked.

"He wanted to know all about you. It seems he just loved your bread!" said Zia Caterina.

"Nothing like it in all Milano, he said," Zia Clorinda told Tony. "Why, I wouldn't be surprised if he wanted to meet you, the way he went on."

"Well, dear ladies, funny you should say that, because he does want to meet me — after Mass on Sunday," said Tony. "His name is Angelo di Milano."

"Imagine that!" the three women exclaimed. *"Che bella fortuna"* — What good luck for you. "And for Serafina!" they whispered to each other.

"And so, Signor Antonio, I would be most
pleased if you and your lovely daughter would come
to Milano as my guests," Angelo said.

"And if you like our city, I would be proud to set
you up in a fine bakery of your own near the Piazza
del Duomo — the cathedral square. Your fame would
be assured, Signor Antonio. I will see to that."

Tony couldn't believe his ears. His dream was
about to come true. "Why, thank you, Signor Angelo.
But please, call me Tony. All my friends do."

"Also Signor Tony," Angelo continued. "The
advantages for your beautiful daughter would be
great. I admit I would not find it unpleasant for
Serafina to sit beside me at my great table as my
wife — the daughter of Tony, the most famous
baker of Milano."

That did it! Tony agreed, and off he and Serafina went with Angelo. Together they walked all the small streets around the cathedral square and visited all the bakeries and pastry shops.

They tasted *torta* — cake — and *biscotti* — cookies — and *pane* — bread. And Tony was depressed. The bread alone was like nothing Tony had ever tasted: bread made out of the finest, whitest flour; bread shaped like pinwheels; bread with seeds of all sorts scattered over the top.

"It is no use, Signor Angelo," said a very sad Tony. "I can never compete with all these fine bakeries and pastry shops. All I can make is bread, and very simple bread at that. I would be the laughingstock of Milano. It is better if Serafina and I just go home."

"No, never!" Angelo shouted.

"Oh, Papa, no," Serafina cried. Not only was she in love with Angelo, but she was looking forward to living in that grand house with all those good things to eat.

"If only you could make bread that tasted as good and sweet as this candied fruit and these raisins," Serafina said.

"Or," Angelo said, getting another idea, "as rich and sweet as this cup of punch made from milk and eggs and honey!"

"Milk, eggs, honey," Tony said, thinking out loud.

"Candied fruit," Serafina said. "Raisins," Angelo chimed in.

"That's it!" all three shouted.

"I shall make the richest, lightest, most wonderful bread anyone has ever tasted — out of the whitest flour, the biggest eggs, the creamiest milk, the sweetest candied fruit and the plumpest raisins," Tony shouted.

"Oh, Papa," Serafina cried, kissing her father.

"Servants," Angelo called, and he sent them off to buy all the fine ingredients Tony would need.

The next morning, Tony, Serafina and all the supplies headed back to the little village.

And Tony began to work. Day after day he experimented until he had mixed the lightest, richest dough with as many raisins and as much candied fruit as he could put into it.

Now he was ready to bake. He sent word to Angelo in Milano that he should come to the bakery the next afternoon.

Then he set out the dough in large bowls and went to bed. As Tony slept, the dough began to rise and rise and rise.

The next morning he filled every pan in his shop. One piece of dough was left over so he threw it in a flower pot and baked it too.

When Angelo arrived, the bread was just coming out of the oven. Everyone held his breath and waited while Tony cut a slice of his new bread. Angelo tasted it. Serafina tasted it. Tony tasted it. Zia Clotilda, Zia Caterina, Zia Clorinda all tasted it.

"That's it!" they shouted.

"I'll take these loaves back to Milano to see what my friends say," Angelo said, and off he went.

In just a few days a letter and a large cart filled with ingredients arrived in the village.

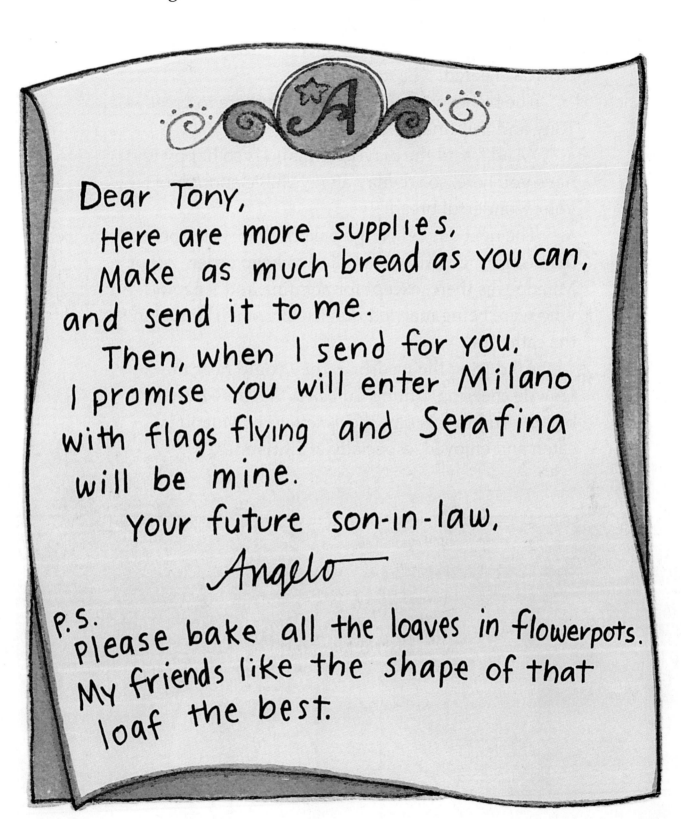

Dear Tony,

Here are more supplies, Make as much bread as you can, and send it to me.

Then, when I send for you, I promise you will enter Milano with flags flying and Serafina will be mine.

Your future son-in-law,

Angelo

P.S. Please bake all the loaves in flowerpots. My friends like the shape of that loaf the best.

Just before Christmas, Angelo sent for Tony and Serafina. Sure enough, when their coach entered Milano, crowds were cheering and flags were flying.

"Benvenuto, Tonio!" — Welcome, Tony! — the crowds cheered. *"Benvenuto!"*

The bishop and the mayor were there to greet Tony and Serafina.

"And," said the mayor, "Milano is so happy to have you here, so we may always have enough of your wonderful bread!"

The next day when the bakery door was opened, the bishop's guards were called to keep order. All of Milano was there, except for Serafina and Angelo, who were being married quietly in a small chapel in the cathedral.

All during the wedding, they could hear the crowds cheering, calling for *pan di Tonio* — Tony's bread. And to this day, the *panettone* of Milano is eaten and enjoyed, especially at Christmas.

BRAVA SERAFINA, BRAVO ANGELO.
BRAVO TONY!

MEET

Tomie dePaola

When he isn't writing and illustrating books such as *Strega Nona* and *The Legend of the Bluebonnet*, Tomie dePaola likes to spend time cooking and baking. His New Hampshire home has two full kitchens plus a grill room especially designed for baking bread and cooking meat. Tomie dePaola has been known to make a batch of *panettone* (pah-nah-TOE-nay) once in a while. There are a total of six ovens in his house. Sometimes, he cooks dinner for as many as thirty friends and uses all six ovens at the same time. *Buon appetito!*

Tomie dePaola in his grill room making an Italian bread called *pane pugliese* (PAH-nay pool-YAY-say)

Fresh Out of the Oven

Create a Commercial

The Best Bread in Town

Tony needs to advertise his new bakery in Milano. Write and act out a commercial in which Tony convinces people to try his *panettone*.

Write a Folktale

Cook Up a Story

Tony's Bread explains how *panettone* was invented. Write a folktale about how another kind of bread was first made. You could choose pizza crust, pita bread, hot dog rolls, or another bread you like.

by Ann Hinga Klein

SANDWICHES from Around THE WORLD

Raise your hand if you like peanut butter and jelly sandwiches. Okay, now raise your hand if you like smoked eel sandwiches.

Just kidding! But did you know that in Holland, some kids really do like smoked eel sandwiches?

Kids around the world eat all kinds of sandwiches. We asked kids and parents from many different countries about the sandwiches they like to eat. Here is what they told us:

ETHIOPIA:

A popular bread called "injera" (in-JER-ah) looks like a big pancake. Ethiopian kids tear injera into pieces and use it to scoop up a reddish meat or vegetable sauce.

SWITZERLAND:

Some kids in Switzerland like strong cheese and salami on bread from a long loaf called a "baguette" (bag-ET).

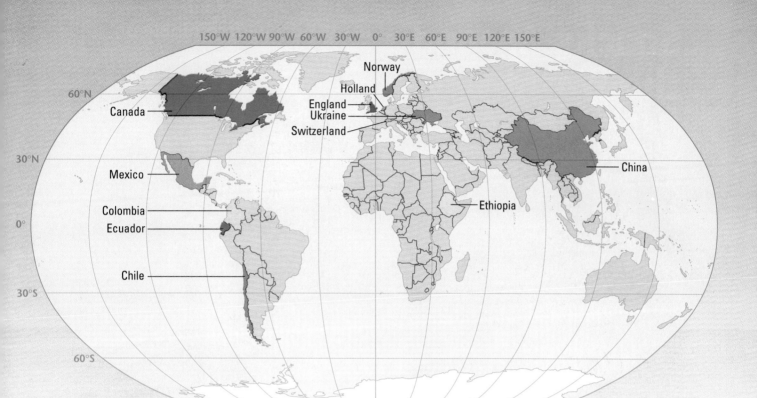

Norway
Holland
England
Ukraine
Switzerland
Canada
Mexico
Colombia
Ecuador
Chile
China
Ethiopia

150°W 120°W 90°W 60°W 30°W 0° 30°E 60°E 90°E 120°E 150°E
60°N
30°N
0°
30°S
60°S

Avocado

ECUADOR:

Pork sandwiches are popular in Ecuador. Inside the bun, you will find a slice of roast pork, a bit of onion, a slice of tomato, lettuce, and some green avocado paste.

CHILE:

If you visit a friend in Chile, you might be served hot dogs with hot mayonnaise. Or your friend might offer you an avocado sandwich with onion. Did you say no thanks? Then how about an "empanada" (emp-in-AH-dah)? An empanada has cheese or meat in the middle, and a crust all around it.

Snacks Around the World

Just like you, kids around the world want snacks when they get hungry between meals.

In **Colombia**, school kids munch potato chips, oranges, or pieces of pineapple.

In **China**, children nibble on popcorn, cookies, candy, or fruit for a treat. They can eat ice cream for a bedtime snack, but never right after a meal. That's because many parents believe that eating warm foods and cold foods at the same time will make their children's stomachs feel sick.

UKRAINE:
Ukranians eat piroshki (per-OSH-kee). A piroshki has potatoes or meat inside and a crust all around the outside. Many Ukranian people like their piroshki hot and spicy.

ENGLAND:
Jam sandwiches are after-school favorites in England. So are sandwiches with chocolate spread. Some English children like cheese-and-cucumber sandwiches. Others want just plain bread with butter.

In **Mexico**, children can buy snow cones in the market. The ice is in a huge block, and a person scrapes off small pieces and puts them in a cup. Kids can choose from 10 or 12 different syrup flavors. Children in Mexico also eat an orange fruit called a mango.

It is served on a stick and covered with hot chile pepper powder!

In **Canada**, children like clementines (CLEM-en-teens). These are sweet little oranges the size of golf balls.

Hot Peppers

MEXICO:

A taco is a sandwich in Mexico. You can buy a pork taco to eat for breakfast. Lunch is a big meal with soup, meat, and beans, but not sandwiches. People do eat sandwiches for supper in Mexico. Some people like roast chicken on thick slices of bread with sliced onions, tomatoes, and hot peppers. In some families, even the little children eat hot peppers.

NORWAY:

How about a sandwich of smoked salmon and scrambled eggs? That's what you might be served in Norway.

About the Author

Sook Nyul Choi grew up in North Korea. As a girl, she loved to read about faraway places, such as the United States. Years later, Sook Nyul Choi moved to the United States and became a teacher and then a writer. She likes to write about her homeland and about Korean people.

About the Illustrator

Karen M. Dugan had a lot of help illustrating *Halmoni and the Picnic*. To draw the setting accurately, she had a friend in New York City take pictures of the streets. She modeled the main character, Yunmi, after the author's own daughters. The author even made a Korean dish called *kimbap* and sent photos of it so Dugan could draw it.

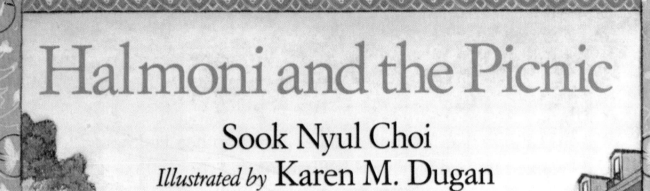

Halmoni and the Picnic

Sook Nyul Choi

Illustrated by Karen M. Dugan

Hand in hand, Yunmi and her grandmother, Halmoni, walked toward St. Patrick's Elementary School. Taxi cabs darted between the big buses rumbling down busy Fourteenth Street. Yunmi squeezed Halmoni's hand and smiled. Halmoni nodded in acknowledgment, but kept her eyes on the street without smiling. Just like the day before, Halmoni looked sad as they drew closer to the school. She did not like going back to their empty apartment all alone.

Miss Stein, in her white uniform, was coming back from working the night shift at Beth Israel Hospital.

"Good morning, Miss Stein!" Yunmi called.

"Oh, hello, Yunmi," said Miss Stein, half smiling and half yawning.

"Yunmi," Halmoni said in Korean, "you must not call out to grown-ups. You should lower your eyes out of respect. It is rude for little ones to disturb their elders!"

Yunmi giggled. "Halmoni, people like it when I greet them. In America it isn't rude to call grown-ups by their names. Here it is rude *not* to say hello and *not* to look people in the eye when you speak to them."

Halmoni sighed. "I will never get used to living here."

Yunmi was sad for her grandmother, who found America too different from Korea.

"Halmoni," she said, "my friends like the bags of fruit you give them each morning."

"I am glad. It is always nice to share with friends," said Halmoni.

"Will you please say hello to my friends in English this morning? They will be so surprised to hear you talk to them. I know you can. Please, Halmoni?"

Halmoni replied, "No, I have only been here for two months. English words are still too difficult for my old tongue. I will sound funny. I will give them this fruit; that is my way of saying hello to them. Besides, you do enough talking for both of us!"

"Yunmi, Yunmi, wait for me!" they heard Anna Marie shout from behind them.

Then Helen came running up from a side street. "Hi, Anna Marie! Hi, Yunmi!"

They said hello to Halmoni. Halmoni nodded and gave one brown bag to each girl.

"Oh, thank you!" said Helen.

"Goody," said Anna Marie. "An apple, grapes, and cherries, too!" The girls said goodbye to Halmoni and headed toward the school yard.

Helen said, "Yunmi, your grandmother is so nice, but she never says anything. Why don't you teach her some English?"

Yunmi shook her head sadly. "My grandmother is embarrassed to speak with an accent. She could speak English if she wanted to. She is smart. She used to be a teacher in Korea."

Helen thought for a while. "Maybe your grandmother is not happy here. When I'm not happy, I don't want to learn anything new. Maybe she's like me."

"That's true. I'm like that, too," Anna Marie agreed.

Yunmi sighed just like Halmoni and said, "I think she's lonely when I'm at school. My parents are so busy working that they have no time for her. I know she misses her old friends, but I don't want her to go back to Korea."

"She needs new friends!" Anna Marie exclaimed. "We can be her friends. We see her every day and we like her."

"We must do something to show her that we want to be her new friends," Helen said with determination. "What can we do?"

They entered the school yard and sat under the big oak tree thinking quietly. That morning they did not play tag or jump rope. When the bell rang, they went to their classroom and unpacked their bookbags in silence.

"Children, I have a special announcement to make this morning," Mrs. Nolan said. "Next Tuesday is our annual picnic in Central Park. We need a chaperon, so please ask your parents if one of them can come and help us."

Helen and Anna Marie raised their arms high, nearly falling off their chairs. Surprised, Mrs. Nolan said, "Yes, Helen, you first. What is it?"

Helen blushed, then asked, "Can Yunmi's grandmother be our chaperon, please?"

Mrs. Nolan said, "Of course. But Yunmi must ask her grandmother first. Will you, Yunmi?"

Helen and Anna Marie grinned and nodded at Yunmi with excitement. But Yunmi was suddenly confused and worried. What if Halmoni did not want to come? What if the children made fun of her pointed rubber shoes or her long Korean dress?

That afternoon Yunmi cautiously told Halmoni what had happened at school.

Halmoni blushed with pleasure. "Helen said that? Your teacher wants me?"

So relieved to see Halmoni looking happy, Yunmi nodded her head up and down.

Touching Yunmi's cheek, Halmoni asked, "And do you want me to go to the picnic with you?"

"Yes, yes, Halmoni, it will be fun. You will meet all my friends, and Mrs. Nolan, and we will be together all day long in Central Park."

"Then yes, I will come," Halmoni said.

Halmoni would not go to the picnic empty-handed. She prepared a huge fruit basket for the third graders. She also insisted on making large plates of kimbap and a big jug of barley tea. Kimbap is made of rice, carrots, eggs, and green vegetables wrapped in seaweed. Again, Yunmi was worried. Most of the children would bring bologna or peanut butter sandwiches, which they would wash down with soda pop. What if no one wanted to eat Halmoni's kimbap? What if they made faces?

"Halmoni, please do not take the kimbap to the picnic. It took you so long to make. Let's save it for us to eat later."

"Oh, it was no problem. It looks so pretty and it's perfect for picnics. I wonder if I made enough."

On the morning of the picnic, Yunmi and her grandmother met the bus at school. Halmoni wore her pale blue skirt and top, called a ch'ima and chogori in Korean, with her white socks and white pointed rubber shoes.

When they arrived at Central Park, Halmoni sat under a big chestnut tree and watched the children play. The children took off their jackets and threw them in front of Halmoni. Smiling, she picked them up, shook off the grass and dirt, and folded each of them neatly. She liked the cool earth beneath her and the ringing laughter of the children.

At lunchtime, Halmoni placed the plates of kimbap on a large blue and white silk table cloth. Mrs. Nolan came over and gasped. "Oh, how beautiful they look! Children, come over and look at this. Yunmi's grandmother made my favorite lunch." Halmoni gave Mrs. Nolan a pair of chopsticks and poured a bit of soy sauce into a small dish. As the children munched on their sandwiches, they gathered around and watched Mrs. Nolan pop the little pieces of kimbap into her mouth.

Halmoni picked up one kimbap with her chopsticks and held it out to Helen. "Mogobwa," she said, which means "Try it." Helen understood and opened her mouth. Everyone watched her expression carefully as she chewed the strange-looking food. Her cautious chewing turned to delight. "Ummm, it's good!"

53

Then, Halmoni picked up another one and held it out for Anna Marie. "Nodo," she said, which means "You too." Anna Marie chewed slowly and then her face brightened, too. Helen and Anna Marie were ready for seconds, and soon everyone was eating the kimbap.

Halmoni smiled, displaying all her teeth. She forgot that in Korea it is not dignified for a woman to smile in public without covering her mouth with her hand.

After lunch, some children asked Halmoni to hold one end of their jump rope. Others asked if Halmoni would make kimbap again for next year's picnic. When Yunmi translated, Halmoni nodded and said, "Kurae, kurae," meaning "Yes, yes."

The children started to chant as they jumped rope:

> "One, two, pointed shoe.
> Three, four, kimbap more.
> Five, six, chopsticks.
> Seven, eight, kimbap plate.
> Kurae, kurae, Picnic Day!"

Halmoni smiled until tears clouded her vision. Her long blue ch'ima danced in the breeze as she turned the jump rope. She tapped her shoes to the rhythm of their song.

Mrs. Nolan asked Yunmi, "What should the class call your grandmother? Mrs. Lee?"

Yunmi said, "I just call her Halmoni, which means grandmother. In Korea, it is rude to call elders by their names."

Mrs. Nolan nodded and smiled. "Children, why don't we all thank Halmoni for her delicious kimbap?"

"Thank you for the kimbap, Halmoni!" the children shouted in unison. Halmoni's wrinkled face turned red and she looked down at her pointed shoes. She took a handkerchief from the large sleeve of her chogori and wiped her eyes.

Halmoni was deep in thought as the big bus wove through the New York City streets. When the bus arrived back at school, the children hurried off, shouting goodbye. Halmoni murmured in English, "Goodbye, goodbye."

Filled with pride, Yunmi grabbed Halmoni's hand and gave it a squeeze. Halmoni squeezed back. Yunmi grinned, thinking of Halmoni's big smile as the children sang about her in Central Park. Skipping along Fourteenth Street, Yunmi hummed the kimbap song.

She thought she heard Halmoni quietly humming along, too.

Try One of These

Plan a Picnic

Let's Get Together

In a small group, plan a class picnic like the one Yunmi's class had. Where would it take place? What kinds of games would you play? Are there any special guests or foods you would like to bring?

Make a Card

Thank you, Halmoni!

Make a thank-you card that Helen or one of Yunmi's other classmates might send to Halmoni. Write a note thanking her for coming to the picnic and for bringing kimbap.

Spaghetti! Spaghetti!

Spaghetti! spaghetti!
you're wonderful stuff,
I love you, spaghetti,
I can't get enough.
You're covered with sauce
and you're sprinkled with cheese,
spaghetti! spaghetti!
oh, give me some more please.

Spaghetti! spaghetti!
piled high in a mound,
you wiggle, you wriggle,
you squiggle around.
There's slurpy spaghetti
all over my plate,
spaghetti! spaghetti!
I think you are great.

Spaghetti! spaghetti!
I love you a lot,
you're slishy, you're sloshy,
delicious and hot.
I gobble you down
oh, I can't get enough,
spaghetti! spaghetti!
you're wonderful stuff.

Jack Prelutsky

59

I'd Never Eat a Beet

Jack Prelutsky

I'd never eat a beet, because
I could not stand the taste,
I'd rather nibble drinking straws,
or fountain pens, or paste,
I'd eat a window curtain
and perhaps a roller skate,
but a beet, you may be certain
would be wasted on my plate.

I would sooner chew on candles
or the laces from my shoes,
or a dozen suitcase handles
were I ever forced to choose,
I would eat a Ping-Pong paddle,
I would eat a Ping-Pong ball,
I might even eat a saddle,
but a beet? No! Not at all.

I would swallow talcum powder
and my little rubber duck,
I'd have doorknobs in my chowder,
I would eat a hockey puck,
I would eat my model rocket
and the socks right off my feet,
I would even eat my pocket,
but I'd never eat a beet!

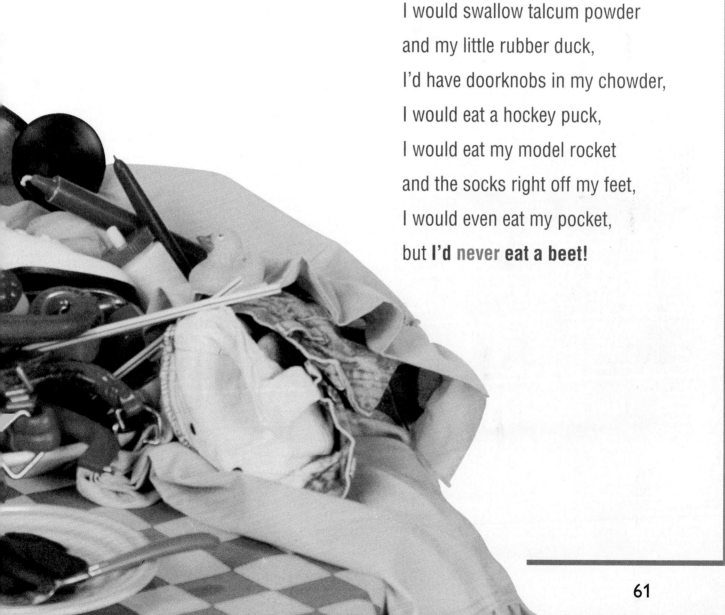

Beverly Cleary

HENRY AND BEEZUS

R I B S Y
and the Roast

HENRY HUGGINS stood by the front window of his square white house on Klickitat Street and wondered why Sunday afternoon seemed so much longer than any other part of the week. Mrs. Huggins was reading a magazine, and Mr. Huggins was reading the funnies in the Sunday *Journal*.

Henry's dog, Ribsy, was asleep in the middle of the living-room rug. As Henry looked at him, he suddenly sat up, scratched hard behind his left ear with his left hind foot, and flopped down again without even bothering to open his eyes.

Henry pressed his nose against the windowpane and looked out at Klickitat Street. The only person he saw was Scooter McCarthy, who was riding up and down the sidewalk on his bicycle.

"I sure wish I had a bike," remarked Henry to his mother and father, as he watched Scooter.

"I wish you did, too," agreed his mother, "but with prices and taxes going up all the time, I'm afraid we can't get you one this year."

"Maybe things will be better next year," said Mr. Huggins, dropping the funnies and picking up the sport section.

Henry sighed. He wanted a bicycle now. He could see himself riding up and down Klickitat Street on a shiny red bike. He would wear his

genuine Daniel Boone coonskin cap with the snap-on
tail, only he wouldn't wear the tail fastened to the hat.
He would tie it to the handle bars so that it would
wave in the breeze as he whizzed along.

"Henry," said Mrs. Huggins, interrupting his
thoughts, "please don't rub your nose against my
clean window."

"All right, Mom," said Henry. "I sure wish
something would happen around here sometime."

"Why don't you go over to Robert's house?
Maybe he can think of something to do," suggested
Mrs. Huggins, as she turned a page of her magazine.

"O.K.," agreed Henry. Robert's mother said they
couldn't give the white mice rides on Robert's electric
train any more, but maybe they could think of
something else. "Come on, Ribsy," said Henry.

Ribsy stood up and shook himself, scattering hair
over the rug.

"That dog," sighed Mrs. Huggins.

Henry thought he had better leave quickly. As he and Ribsy started down the front steps, Robert came around the corner.

"What's up, Doc?" said Robert.

"Hi," responded Henry.

"My dad said maybe if I came over to your house, you could think of something to do," said Robert.

The boys sat down on the front steps. "Here comes old Scooter," observed Robert. The two boys watched the older boy pumping down the street on his bicycle. He was whistling, and not only was he riding without touching the handle bars, he even had his hands in his pockets.

"Hi," said Scooter casually, without stopping.

"Big show-off," muttered Robert. "I bet he takes that bike to bed with him."

"He sure thinks he's smart," agreed Henry. "He's been riding up and down all afternoon. Come on, let's go around in the back yard, where we won't have to watch old Scooter show off all day. Maybe we can find something to do back there."

Ribsy followed at the boys' heels. Unfortunately, the back yard was no more interesting than the front. The only sign of life was next door. A large yellow cat was dozing on the Grumbies' back steps, and there was smoke coming from the barbecue pit.

Robert looked thoughtful. "Does Ribsy ever chase cats?"

"Not that old Fluffy." Henry, understanding what was on Robert's mind, explained that Mrs. Grumbie sprinkled something called Doggie-B-Gone

65

on her side of the rosebushes. Ribsy disliked the
smell of it and was careful to stay on his side of the
bushes.

Robert was disappointed. "I thought Ribsy
might . . ."

"No such luck," interrupted Henry, looking at his
dog, who had settled himself by the back steps to
continue his nap. Henry picked a blade of grass and
started to blow through it when the squeak-slam of
the Grumbies' screen door made him look up.
"Jeepers!" he whispered.

Stepping carefully over Fluffy, Mr. Hector
Grumbie walked down the back steps. He was

wearing a chef's tall white hat and an immense white apron. *What's cooking?* was written across the hat, and on the apron was printed a recipe for *Bar X Ranch Bar-B-Q Sauce.* Mr. Grumbie carried a tray full of bowls, jars, bottles, and what appeared to be bunches of dried weeds.

"Is he really going to cook?" whispered Robert.

"Search me," answered Henry. The two boys edged closer to the rosebushes that divided the two yards.

"Hello, Mr. Grumbie," said Henry.

"Hello there, Henry." Mr. Grumbie crossed the lawn and set the tray on the edge of the barbecue pit in the corner of his yard. He peeled a small object which he put into a bowl, sprinkled with salt, and mashed with a little wooden stick. Then he broke off pieces of the dried weeds and mashed them, too.

Henry and Robert exchanged puzzled looks.

"Need any help, Mr. Grumbie?" asked Henry.

"No, thank you." Mr. Grumbie poured a few drops of something into the mixture.

"Is that something that's supposed to be good to eat?" asked Robert. Mr. Grumbie didn't answer.

"What's that stuff in the bowl?" asked Henry.

"Herbs and garlic," answered Mr. Grumbie. "Now run along and play, boys. I'm busy."

Henry and Robert did not move.

"Etta!" called Mr. Grumbie to his wife. "I forgot the vinegar." He coughed as a breeze blew smoke in his face.

"I'll go get it for you," offered Henry, but his neighbor ignored him.

Squeak-slam went the screen. Mrs. Grumbie stepped over Fluffy and walked across the yard with a bottle in her hand. "Hector, can't we take your friends out to dinner instead of going to all this trouble?" she asked, as she fanned smoke out of her eyes.

"This is no trouble at all." Mr. Grumbie added a few drops of vinegar to the mixture in the bowl.

Henry thought Mrs. Grumbie looked cross, as she said, "Hector, why don't you let me cook the meat in the house? It would be so much easier and then we could bring it outside to eat."

"Now, Etta, I know what I'm doing." Mr. Grumbie poured a few drops from another bottle and mashed some more.

"But I don't like to see you spoil the flavor of a perfectly good piece of meat with all that seasoning. It

would be different if you really knew how to cook."
Mrs. Grumbie frowned, as she swatted at a bug circling over the sauce.

Mr. Grumbie frowned even more. "Anyone who can read a recipe can cook."

Mrs. Grumbie's face turned red, as she clapped the bug between her hands, and said sharply, "Oh, is that so? What about the time you cut up tulip bulbs in the hamburgers because you thought they were onions?"

"That," said Mr. Grumbie, even more sharply, "was different."

Mrs. Grumbie angrily fanned smoke with her apron. "Just remember when we try to eat this mess you're fixing that it wasn't my idea. Even if the recipe is any good, the meat will probably be burned on the outside and raw inside. Smoke will get in our eyes and we'll be eaten alive by mosquitoes and . . ."

Mr. Grumbie interrupted. "Etta, we won't argue about it any more. I invited my friends to a barbecue and we're going to have a barbecue."

Henry and Robert were disappointed. They hoped the Grumbies would argue about it a lot more.

Then Mr. Grumbie looked at the recipe printed on his apron. Because he was looking down at it, the words were upside down for him. "What does it say here?" he asked, pointing to his stomach.

Henry and Robert could not help snickering.

"Now, boys, run along and don't bother us. We're busy," said Mrs. Grumbie.

"Come on, Robert."

Henry turned away from the rosebushes. He felt uncomfortable around Mrs. Grumbie, because he thought she didn't like him. At least, she didn't like

Ribsy and that was the same as not liking Henry. He didn't want to make her any crosser than she was already, although secretly he couldn't see why she minded Ribsy's burying a bone in her pansy bed once in a while.

Henry tried standing on his hands just to show Mrs. Grumbie he wasn't paying any attention to what she was doing. Then he heard someone coming up his driveway. It was his friend Beezus and her little sister Ramona, who lived in the next block on Klickitat Street. Beezus' real name was Beatrice, but Ramona called her Beezus, and so did everyone else. Beezus was carrying a baton and Ramona was riding a shiny new tricycle.

"Whoa!" yelled Ramona to her tricycle. Then she got off and tied it to a bush with a jumping rope.

"Hello," said Beezus. "See my baton."

The boys examined the metal rod, which was about two and a half feet long with a rubber knob at each end.

"What are you going to do with it?" asked Henry.

"Twirl it," said Beezus.

"I'll bet," scoffed Robert.

"I am too," said Beezus. "I take lessons every Saturday. By June I'll be good enough so I can twirl it in the Junior Rose Festival parade, and some day I'm going to be a drum majorette."

"June is only a couple of months away," said Henry, wondering what he would do in the parade this year. "Let's see you twirl it."

Beezus held the baton over her head and started to turn it with her right hand. It slipped from her fingers and hit her on the head.

"Boi-i-ing!" shouted the two boys together.

"You keep quiet," said Beezus crossly.

"Let me try," said Henry.

"No," answered Beezus, whose feelings were hurt.

"I didn't want to anyway." Henry started across the yard. "Come on, Robert, let's climb the cherry tree."

"All right for you, Henry Huggins!" shouted Beezus, as the boys scrambled up through the branches. "I'm going home. Come on, Ramona, untie your horse."

But Ramona had seen Ribsy and she began to pat him on the head. Ribsy groaned in his sleep and sat up to scratch. Suddenly he was wide awake, sniffing the air.

"Wuf!" said Ribsy.

Henry could tell by the sound of the bark that Ribsy was excited about something. He peered out through the leaves of the cherry tree, but could see nothing unusual in his back yard. He saw Ribsy stand up, shake himself, and trot purposefully toward the Grumbies' back yard, with Ramona running after him.

Henry looked across the rosebushes and groaned at what he saw. On a platter beside the barbecue pit was a large piece of raw meat. The Grumbies were nowhere in sight.

"Here, Ribsy! Come here, boy!" called Henry frantically, but Ribsy did not stop. "Catch him, Beezus!"

Ramona, who was trying to follow Ribsy through the rosebushes, shrieked.

"Hold still," directed Beezus, struggling with her little sister. "I can't get you loose from all these thorns when you wiggle that way."

"Come on, we better be getting out of here." Henry slipped and slid down the tree. "I bet the rain washed off the Doggie-B-Gone."

"I guess we better," agreed Robert cheerfully. After all, Ribsy wasn't his dog.

Henry hit the ground and tried to run through the rosebushes. Thorns clawed at his jeans and held him fast. "Here, Ribsy," he yelled. "Here, Ribs, old boy!"

Ribsy jumped for the roast.

With one desperate jerk, Henry tried to free himself from the roses. The thorns dug deeper into his legs.

Ribsy sank his teeth into the meat and pulled it to the ground.

Mr. Grumbie came through the back door with an armload of kindling. "Hey, stop that dog!" he yelled, dropping the wood on his toe. "Ow!" he groaned, as he started toward Ribsy and stepped on Fluffy's tail.

An ear-splitting yowl brought Mrs. Grumbie to the back porch. "Fluffy," she cooed, "did the man step on the precious pussycat's tail?"

Ribsy paused to take a firmer grip on the roast.

"If that cat hasn't any more sense than to sleep on the steps . . ." snapped Mr. Grumbie. "Hey, make that dog come back here!"

"Oh, my goodness!" exclaimed Mrs. Grumbie, when she saw what had happened. "Here, Ribsy, here, Ribsy!"

That was just what Ribsy needed to make him start running. He didn't like Mrs. Grumbie. He knew she sprinkled Doggie-B-Gone on the shrubbery to keep him away.

With one final yank and the sound of ripping cloth, Henry jerked away from the bushes.

"Tackle him," yelled Robert, who was still trying to untangle himself from the thorns.

Henry flung himself at his dog, but Ribsy raced on. Henry picked himself up off the Grumbies' driveway and ran after him.

Around the Grumbies' house he ran and on down Klickitat Street. He could hear Robert's and Mr. Grumbie's feet pounding down the sidewalk after him.

"Ribsy!" yelled Henry.

"Hey, come back here," shouted Robert.

"Stop thief!" bellowed Mr. Grumbie, holding onto his tall white hat with one hand.

Doors and windows began to open. "What's cooking, Grumbie?" someone called out.

Henry heard his mother say, "Oh, that dog!"

"Henry!" shouted Mr. Huggins.

"Go get 'em, Grumbie," yelled the man across the street.

Mr. Grumbie paused for breath. "Somebody head him off," he directed.

Ribsy ran into the street. A car turned the corner.

"Ribsy," wailed Henry, afraid to look.

"Hey, look out," warned Robert.

The car slammed on its brakes. Ribsy ran back to the sidewalk.

If only Henry could put on a burst of speed and make a really good flying tackle. But no matter how fast he ran, Ribsy was just out of his reach. He glanced over his shoulder and saw that Mr. Grumbie's face was red and he had lost his hat.

"Come . . . here . . . sir!" panted Mr. Grumbie. He wasn't used to running. Then his footsteps grew slower and slower until they stopped altogether.

Henry ran on, with Robert close behind. Their friend Mary Jane came out of her house and

started down the sidewalk toward them. If only she would stop Ribsy. "Catch him!" yelled Henry.

When Ribsy was only a few feet from Mary Jane, he dropped the meat on the sidewalk. Here was her chance. "Get it, Mary Jane," Henry shouted, with almost all the breath he had left. "Get the meat!"

Mary Jane stood staring at Ribsy. "Pick up the meat, you dope!" yelled Robert.

Still Mary Jane did not move. Ribsy waited until Henry was almost within tackling distance before taking a firm grip on the roast and starting to run again.

"Mary Jane," panted Henry, "head him off."

Mary Jane stepped aside and Ribsy ran on. Henry felt as if he could not move another step. "Why didn't you grab the meat?" he demanded, as he paused to catch his breath.

"You could have caught him if you wanted to," accused Robert.

"I couldn't either stop your dirty old dog," said Mary Jane. "Can't you see I'm wearing my Sunday School dress?"

"Mary Jane, you give me a pain." Henry glared at her.

"You're a poet and don't know it," said Mary Jane, twirling around to show off her full skirt.

Robert and Henry looked at one another. Girls!

76

Robert clutched Henry's arm and pointed in the direction from which Ribsy had come. "Look!"

A police dog, a fox terrier, and a sort of collie were running down Klickitat Street toward Ribsy. Now there would be a dog fight, and the roast would be torn to pieces, and the two big dogs would chew up Ribsy. They would probably chew the fox terrier, too, and Henry knew the lady who owned him was very particular about keeping him out of dog fights. Henry would be blamed because the big dogs bit the little dog and . . . Suddenly Henry found he was too tired to do much of anything. He picked up a clod of dirt and threw it at the dogs as they passed him. "Beat it," he said, but he didn't bother to shout. He knew it was no use.

"Boy, a dog fight!" Robert was delighted. "This is going to be keen."

"Aw, keep quiet," said Henry. Robert wouldn't feel that way if Ribsy were his dog. The sort of collie was gaining on Ribsy, and the police dog was not far behind. Poor Ribsy! Henry shut his eyes. He couldn't stand seeing Ribsy chewed to pieces.

"Gangway everybody!" It was Scooter's voice. Leaning over his handle bars and pumping as hard as he could, he tore down the street behind the three dogs. He passed Henry and Robert and, swerving to avoid the dogs, caught up with Ribsy. He didn't stop for the curb, but rode right over it with a tremendous bump. Then he flung himself off the bicycle and on top of Ribsy before the dog knew what was happening.

Ribsy dropped the meat and Scooter snatched it. He sprang on his bicycle, wheeled around in the middle of the street, and started back toward the Grumbies' house, holding the meat above his head with one

hand. The three other dogs and Ribsy all chased after
Scooter, barking and growling as they jumped up and
tried to snap at the meat.

Eluding them all, Scooter pedaled triumphantly
back down Klickitat Street. "Hi," he said briefly to
Henry and Robert, as he passed them.

"Hey, give me that meat," demanded Henry.
Scooter ignored him.

"How do you like that!" said Robert. "He sure
thinks he's smart."

Henry ran after Scooter, who pedaled even faster.
Henry put on a burst of speed. So did Scooter. So did
the dogs. Henry could hear the neighbors laughing.
He tried to run faster, but Scooter stayed just out of
his reach.

When Scooter reached the Grumbies' house, he
handed the meat to its owner. "There you are, Mr.
Grumbie," he said.

Mr. Grumbie took the battered roast. "Thank you, Scooter. That was mighty quick thinking on your part."

"It wasn't anything," said Scooter modestly. "It was easy to catch up with him on my bike."

The other dogs lost interest and ran away, but Ribsy continued to whimper and jump for the meat. Then even he gave up and sat panting, with his long pink tongue hanging out.

Poor Ribsy, thought Henry. He wanted that meat so much. Maybe he's tired of horse meat. Henry wished he dared to pet his dog, even though he had been cross with him.

"He's a dumb dog," said Scooter. "It's a good thing I came along and saved him from those other dogs when I did."

"I think you're mean, Scooter McCarthy," said Beezus. "Poor Ribsy."

"Why don't you go home?" said Henry to Scooter.

"Now, children," said Mrs. Huggins. Then she said to Mrs. Grumbie, "You must let us buy you another roast. Henry can help pay for it out of his allowance. He knows he is supposed to keep his dog out of your yard."

"Gee, my mother says roasts are expensive," said Scooter.

"You keep quiet." Henry scowled at Scooter. Why was Scooter always around when things happened to him? "Jeepers, I'm sorry, Mrs. Grumbie," said Henry. "I don't know what got into Ribsy. He was just hungry, I guess."

"He always is," observed Mr. Huggins.

Meat markets were closed on Sunday, but Henry knew that the delicatessen counter in the Supermarket was open. "Delicatessens have wienies, don't they?" he asked. "I could run down to the Supermarket and get some for you, if you'd like."

"I could go faster on my bike," said Scooter.

Mrs. Grumbie smiled. "Thank you, Henry. That won't be necessary. I think we'll go out to dinner." She looked at Mr. Grumbie, who had started toward the house with the roast. "Just between you and me," she whispered, "I don't think the meat would have been fit to eat with that sauce Mr. Grumbie was going to put on it." Then she called to her husband, "Hector, what are you going to do with that dirty piece of meat?"

"I suppose he might as well have it," said Mr. Grumbie reluctantly. "Not that he deserves it." He threw the remains to Ribsy.

Mrs. Grumbie paused in the doorway. "Henry, I'm going to bake cookies tomorrow. If you'll stop by on your way home from school tomorrow, I'll give you some."

"Thank you, Mrs. Grumbie," answered Henry. She seemed almost glad Ribsy had stolen the roast. At least, she wasn't cross any more.

"Here, Ribsy, it isn't time for you to eat yet." Henry tugged at the roast, but Ribsy hung on and growled. "Come on, Dad, give me a hand."

Mr. Huggins took hold of the meat and together they got it away from Ribsy. "I'll put it in the refrigerator for him," said Mr. Huggins, "and I'll have a talk with you later."

"Aw, gee, Dad," protested Henry. "I wasn't doing anything."

"You wanted something to happen, didn't you?" said Mr. Huggins, as he carried the meat into the house.

Henry did not answer. He just sighed and sat down on the steps. Why did these things always have to happen to him, anyway?

About the Author
Beverly Cleary

Beverly Cleary grew up in Portland, Oregon, just a few blocks away from Klickitat Street. She thinks her books about Henry and his friends have become popular because they're about ordinary boys and girls — "children who play together and whose parents sometimes do not have enough money but who manage somehow."

About the Illustrator
Alan Tiegreen

Alan Tiegreen says he has "the best job in the world" — illustrating books. Before he begins a new book, he acts out the story and pretends he's the characters he's going to draw. Tiegreen has illustrated several other books by Beverly Cleary, including *Ramona the Brave* and *Ramona Quimby, Age 8.*

If you're ever in Beverly Cleary's hometown of Portland, Oregon, be sure to visit Grant Park. There you'll find life-size statues of Henry, Ribsy, and Ramona. Above, the bronze figures are shown in the studio of sculptor Lee Hunt. Hunt says she modeled Ramona after a photograph of Beverly Cleary at age five.

Where's the Beef?

Ribsy on the Run

Ribsy takes us on an adventure through Henry's neighborhood. Make a map that shows Ribsy's route. Be sure to include all the houses and streets that appear in the story.

What Would Ribsy Say?

Retell the events of the story from another character's point of view. How might Ribsy tell the story? What about Mr. Grumbie?

Get the Facts On FAST FOODS

You're watching TV when a commercial comes on. A popular fast-food restaurant tempts you with one of its specials. The camera closes in on a big, juicy burger — two meat patties layered with bacon and oozing with melted cheese.

Your mouth starts watering. You suddenly feel hungry. How could anyone resist?

People buy fast foods for several reasons. They're tasty, quick, convenient, and don't cost too much. It's easy to pick up a sausage biscuit on your way to school or grab a cheeseburger when you don't have time for a regular meal.

But there are some important things you should know about fast food and the part it plays in your daily diet.

Choose or Lose

The federal government offers simple guidelines to help you choose foods that nourish your body and keep you healthy. These guidelines are known as the Food Guide Pyramid.

At the base of the pyramid is the bread, cereal, rice, and pasta group. These foods are the basis for a healthy diet, and six to 11 servings a day are highly recommended.

Next come those important fruits and vegetables. We should eat two to four servings of fruits and three to five servings of vegetables each day.

Dairy foods (like milk, cheese, and yogurt) and protein foods (like meat, poultry, fish, dry beans, eggs, and nuts) form the next level on the pyramid. We need two to three servings of both dairy foods and protein foods each day.

At the very top of the pyramid are fats, oils, and sweets. While we like the taste, these foods are high in calories and fat and low in nutritional value. That means they should be eaten in small quantities.

And that's where we run into a problem with fast foods. Many of the most popular are very high in fat. Deep-frying foods, like potatoes or onion rings, chicken pieces or chicken nuggets, and fish fillets adds fats. Adding cheese and processed meats, like bacon and sausage, also adds a lot of fat.

The Fault of Fat

The problem with the fat in fast foods is that it is usually *saturated* (sat´-ū-rāt-ed) — the kind of fat that can increase the cholesterol level in your blood. Many studies have shown that can cause arteries to clog and get in the way of normal blood flow.

What's more, many fast foods contain a great deal of sodium (salt) and sugar.

Let's say you order a quarter-pound cheeseburger, large order of fries, chocolate shake, and apple pie. That meal contains 1,560 calories, 17 teaspoons of fat, and 1,640 milligrams of sodium. This is far more than anyone needs — especially at one meal.

That fast-food meal contains more than half of the total calories needed for the whole day.

So, does this mean that we have to cut out all fast foods if we want to be healthy and fit?

Of course not. You don't have to cut out the fun, convenience, and taste of fast foods — if you learn to make smart choices. And many fast-food restaurants now offer more healthy foods.

Fast-Food Good News

You can choose healthy fast foods. Here are some tips:

🍎 Stay away from regularly eating deep-fried foods. Choose broiled, grilled, or roasted sandwiches instead of breaded and deep-fried.

🍎 Hold the sauces. Hidden fat and calories hide in the mayo, tartar sauce, and dressings.

🍎 Watch your toppings. A good choice in fast food is a baked potato. But go easy on the cheese, butter, and sour cream.

🍎 Stay away from processed meats. Shift to plain burgers, and try pizza with veggies like mushrooms, green peppers, and onions.

🍎 Head for the salad bar. Load up on lettuce, spinach, tomatoes, carrots, broccoli, and mushrooms. Skip the croutons and bacon bits.

🍎 Instead of a regular shake or sugary soda, order low-fat milk or fruit juice.

🍎 End with a winner. Top off your meal with frozen yogurt.

Get in the habit of healthy eating. It's one habit you'll never want to break!

Oranges
A Research Report by Cristina Vela

Did you know that some oranges are red inside?
Cristina learned this fact when she researched
information for her report.

Oranges

The orange is a popular citrus fruit that is eaten around the
world. There are three types of oranges: 1) sweet oranges, 2) sour
or bitter oranges, and 3) mandarins. The sweet orange is the most
popular of all.

Oranges come in different shapes and colors from round to
oval and from pink to orange to dark red in color. Some are even
seedless. The orange tree has dark green, leathery leaves and
beautiful, fragrant flowers.

Oranges grow best where summers are warm and winters are
cool but not too cold. A freeze can kill them or damage the tree
and the fruit. Brazil grows more oranges than any other country.
Most oranges in the United States are grown in Florida, California,
Arizona, and Texas. Spain, Mexico, China, and Italy also grow
oranges.

Growing oranges can involve problems, such as cold weather
and insects. When cold weather comes, farmers may sprinkle water on
the trees to keep them from freezing. In California, wind machines

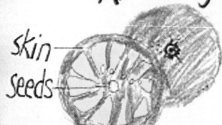

An orange

skin

seeds

The orange
tree

are sometimes used to bring warmer air down to the orchards. Insecticides keep aphids and other bugs from eating the oranges and the leaves.

When the orange is ripe, it is handpicked. Then it goes to a packing plant where it is washed and then dried. Ones that have too many marks on their skins are sent to another plant to be made into juice. The very best oranges are waxed and dried again. Then they pass through machines that stamp them and separate them by size. Finally, they are put into boxes.

It takes a lot of work to produce the oranges that people like to eat.

Bibliography

"Orange." <u>Britannica Junior Encyclopedia</u>. 1979 ed.

"Orange." <u>The World Book Encyclopedia</u>. 1993 ed.

Rogow, Zack. <u>Oranges</u>. New York: Orchard, 1988.

Silverstein, Alvin and Virginia B. <u>Oranges: All About Them</u>. Englewood Cliffs: Prentice, 1975.

Cristina Vela
E. A. Jones Elementary School
Missouri City, Texas

Cristina wrote this report in her third grade social studies class. She also likes to write stories. Cristina enjoys reading, math, and social studies. For fun she likes to play with her younger brother and watch television. Someday Cristina wants to be a teacher.

Meet Patricia Polacco

As a young girl, Patricia Polacco spent many evenings in front of the fireplace, popping corn and listening to her grandmother's stories. Her family called this "firetalking."

Today Polacco writes and illustrates her own stories, many of which are based on family memories. *Chicken Sunday* is about her friendship with Stewart and Winston, two neighborhood boys who are still her best friends today.

On this page, Patricia Polacco in her art studio. **At right**, the finished book with original artwork from the story.

Chicken Sunday
Patricia Polacco

Stewart and Winston were my neighbors. They were my brothers by a solemn ceremony we had performed in their backyard one summer. They weren't the same religion as I was. They were Baptists. Their gramma, Eula Mae Walker, was my gramma now. My babushka had died two summers before.

Sometimes my mother let me go to church on Sunday with them. How we loved to hear Miss Eula sing. She had a voice like slow thunder and sweet rain.

We'd walk to church and back. She'd take my hand as we crossed College Avenue. "Even though we've been churchin' up like decent folks ought to," she'd say, "I don't want you to step in front of one of those too fast cars. You'll be as flat as a hen's tongue." She squeezed my hand.

When we passed Mr. Kodinski's hat shop, Miss Eula would always stop and look in the window at the wonderful hats. Then she'd sigh and we'd walk on.

We called those Sundays "Chicken Sundays" because Miss Eula almost always fried chicken for dinner. There'd be collard greens with bacon, a big pot of hoppin' john, corn on the cob, and fried spoon bread.

One Sunday at the table we watched her paper fan flutter back and forth, pulling moist chicken-fried air along with it. She took a deep breath. Her skin glowed as she smiled. Then she told us something we already knew. "That Easter bonnet in Mr. Kodinski's window is the most beautiful I ever did see," she said thoughtfully.

The three of us exchanged looks. We wanted to get her that hat more than anything in the world.

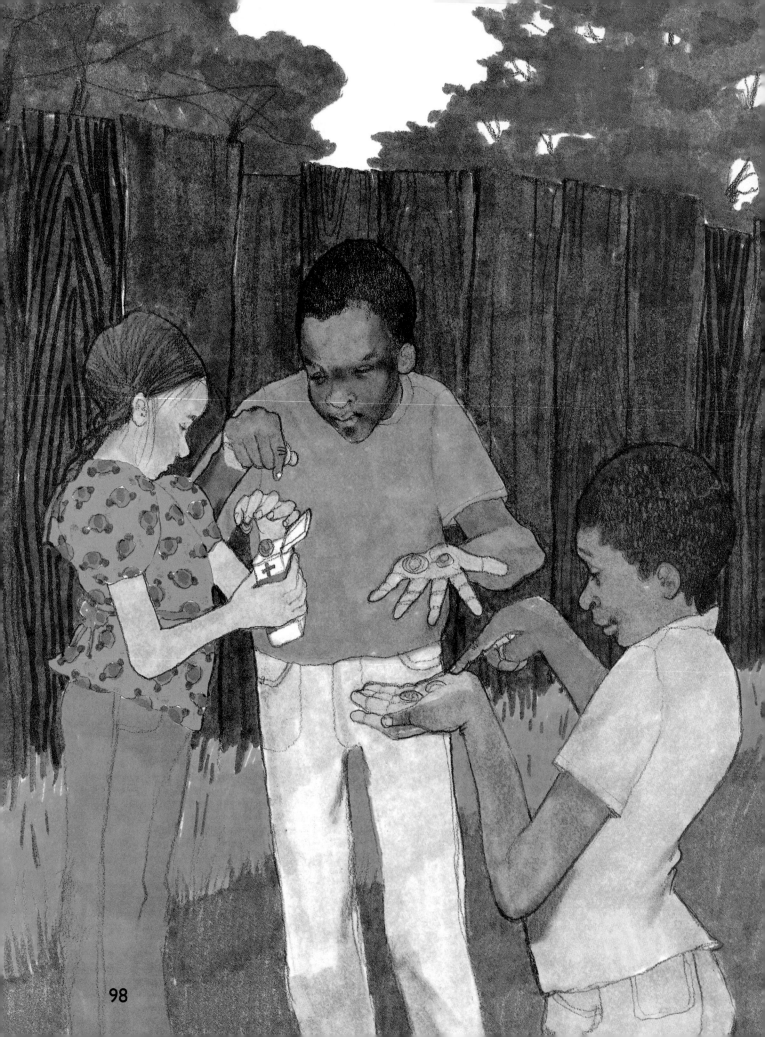

Stewart reached into the hole in the trunk of our "wish tree" in the backyard. He pulled out a rusty Band-Aid tin. The three of us held our breath as we counted the money inside that we had been saving for weeks.

"If we are going to get that hat for Miss Eula in time for Easter, we are going to need a lot more than this," I announced.

"Maybe we should ask Mr. Kodinski if we could sweep up his shop or something to earn the rest of the money," Stewart said.

"I don't know," Winnie said fearfully. "He's such a strange old man. He never smiles at anyone. He always looks so mean!" We all agreed that it was worth a try anyway.

The next day we took a shortcut down the alley in back of the hat shop. Bigger boys were there. They were yelling. Eggs flew past us and pelted Mr. Kodinski's back door.

Just as the boys ran away the door flew open. Mr. Kodinski glared straight at us! "You there," he yelled. "Why do you kids do things like this?"

"It wasn't us," Stewart tried to say, but Mr. Kodinski wouldn't listen to us.

"All I want to do is live my life in peace. I'm calling your grandmother," he shouted as he wagged his finger in Stewart's face.

Miss Eula was waiting in her living room for us. "Miss Eula, we didn't throw those eggs," I sobbed.

"Some big boys did," Stewart sputtered.

"What were you doing at the back of his shop in the first place?" she asked. We knew that we couldn't tell her the truth, so we just stood there and cried.

She looked at us for a long while. "Baby dears, I want to believe you. Heaven knows that I brought you children up to always tell the truth. If you say you didn't do it, then I believe you."

"It is too bad though," she went on to say. "That poor man has suffered so much in his life, he deserves more than eggs thrown at him. You know, he thinks *you* threw the eggs. You'll have to show him that you are good people. You'll have to change his mind somehow."

In my kitchen the next day we thought and
thought.

"How can we win him over when he thinks that
we threw those eggs?" Stewart asked.

"He doesn't even like us," Winston chirped.

"Eggs," I said quietly.

"Eggs?" Stewart asked.

"Eggs!" I screamed.

I went to the kitchen drawer and took out a lump
of beeswax, a candle, a small funnel with a wooden
handle, and some packets of yellow, red, and black dye.

Mom helped me show the boys how to decorate eggs the way my bubbie had taught us. The way they do it in the old country. We made designs on the egg shells with hot wax, then dyed them and finally melted the wax patterns off.

We put the eggs in a basket and, even though we were afraid, marched into Mr. Kodinski's shop and put them on the counter.

He raised his eyebrows and glowered at us. Then his eyes dropped to the basket.

"*Spaseeba,*" he said softly. That means "thank you" in Russian. "Pysanky eggs!" he said as he looked closely. "I haven't seen these since I left my homeland."

"We didn't throw those eggs at your door, Mr. Kodinski," we told him.

He looked at us for a minute. "Well, then, you have great courage to be here. Chutzpah, you have chutzpah!" Then his eyes glistened and his mouth curled into a warm smile. "Come, have some tea with me."

We spent the whole afternoon talking together, having poppy-seed cake and strong tea. He told us about his life. We told him about ours.

When we finally got the courage to ask about doing odd jobs to earn some extra money, he apologized and told us that there was no work. We didn't tell him what we wanted the money for. It didn't seem the right thing to do. Our hearts sank.

"I tell you this," he said thoughtfully. "These eggs are as beautiful as my hats."

Stewart, Winnie, and I looked at each other.

"It is almost Easter," he went on to say. "I'm sure that people would love these eggs. Set up a table and sell them right there in my shop!"

For the next few days we worked very hard. We made almost a dozen "Pysanky" eggs. When people came in, they picked them up and said things like, "Beautiful!" "Splendid!" "Intricate!" "Glorious!" We sold them all in one single day.

That afternoon when all the eggs were gone, we counted our money. We had more than enough for the hat.

Just as we were about to tell Mr. Kodinski that we wanted to buy the hat, he came out from the back room holding a beautiful hatbox . . . gift-wrapped! "Keep your money, children," he said softly. "I have seen Miss Eula admire this. It is for her, isn't it? Tell her that I know you are very good children, such good children!"

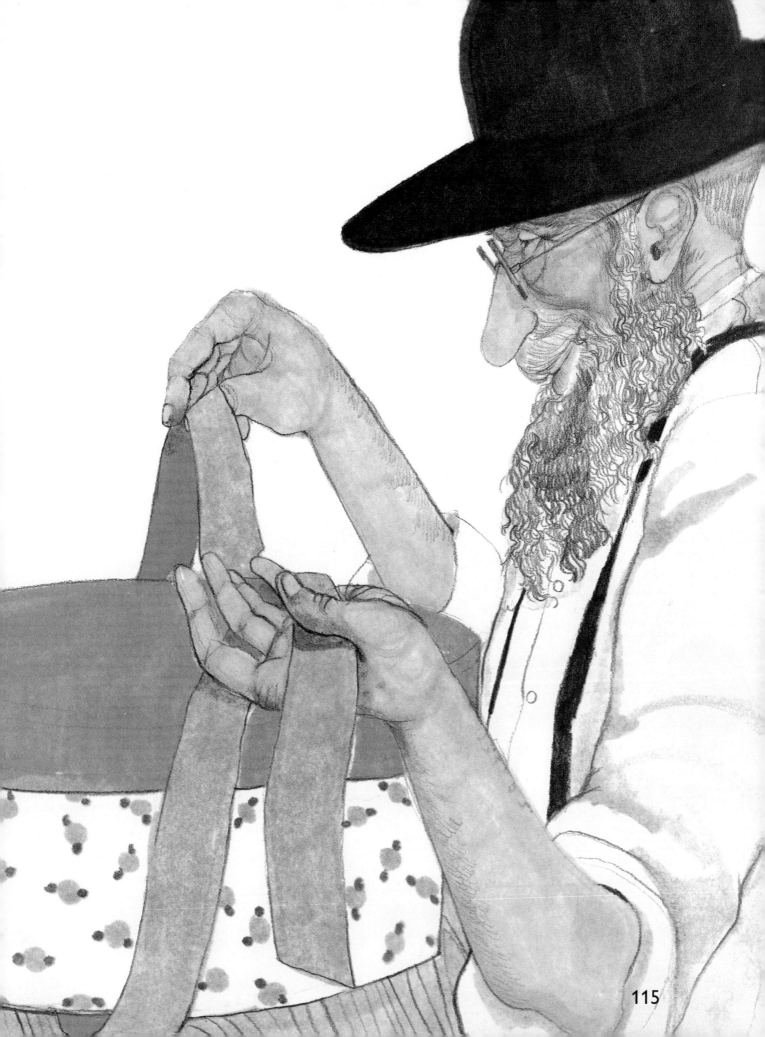

When Easter Sunday arrived, we thought our hearts would burst when we watched Miss Eula open the hatbox. She held us close, as big tears rolled down her cheeks.

Our hearts sang along with the choir that Sunday. She looked so beautiful in that hat. When it was time for her solo, we knew that she was singing just for us.

Her voice was like slow thunder and sweet rain.

Later that day as Miss Eula sat at the head of the table she said, "Oh baby dears, I can die happy now. And after I'm dead, on Chicken Sundays, I want you to boil up some chicken — bones, gravy, and all — and pour it over my grave. So late at night when I'm hungry, I can reach right out and have me some."

Then she rolled her head back and laughed from a deep, holy place inside.

Winston, Stewart, and I are grown up now. Our old neighborhood has changed some, yet it's still familiar, too. The freeway rumbles over the spot where Mr. Kodinski's shop once stood. I think of him often and his glorious hats.

We lost Miss Eula some time back, but every year we take some chicken soup up to Mountain View Cemetery and do just as she asked.

Sometimes, when we are especially quiet inside, we can hear singing. A voice that sounds like slow thunder and sweet rain.

Beautiful!
Splendid!
Glorious!

Make an Advertisement

Eggs for Sale!

Make a poster for Mr. Kodinski's store that advertises the pysanky eggs. Include a picture of the eggs and use descriptive words like those found in the story.

Share a Memory

Show Me How

Patricia Polacco's bubbie taught her how to make pysanky eggs. Talk about something you learned how to do from a friend or family member.

121

Fun Food Facts

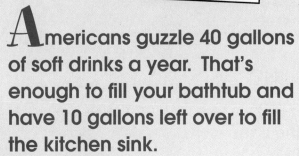

Americans guzzle 40 gallons of soft drinks a year. That's enough to fill your bathtub and have 10 gallons left over to fill the kitchen sink.

Average Americans eat nearly 2,000 pounds of food a year — that's as much as the weight of a small two-door car.

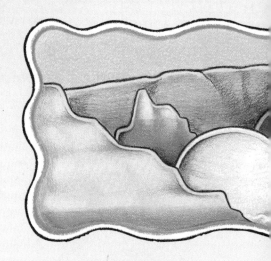

Each year, enough ice cream is produced in the United States to fill the Grand Canyon. The average American eats 15 gallons of ice cream per year — that would fill a washing machine.

Popcorn is a popular fast food. Nationwide, the average person eats 56 quarts of the fluffy stuff each year. That's enough to fill a tall wastebasket to overflowing.

Americans eat 19 billion hot dogs each year. If you laid them end to end, they would go around the world 60 times!

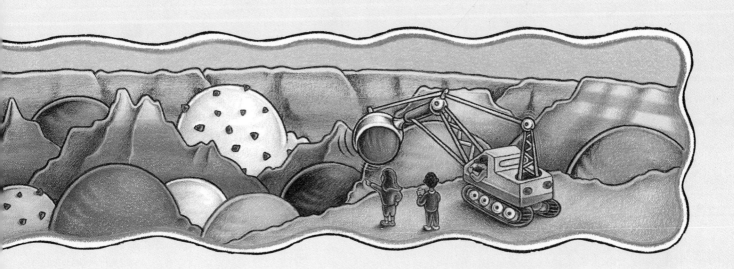

Weather Watch

Weather Watch Contents

Kate Shelley and the *Midnight Express*

by Margaret K. Wetterer
illustrations by Karen Ritz

PAPERBACK PLUS

Kate Shelley and the *Midnight Express*
by Margaret K. Wetterer
The river is flooded, the bridge is out, and a train is fast approaching! Read what happens in this true adventure story.

In the same book . . .
Information about steam engines, the real Kate Shelley, and more.

PAPERBACK **PLUS**

Yagua Days
by Cruz Martel
What do you do on a rainy day? If you live in Puerto Rico, rainy days can be wonderful days if they're *yagua* days.

In the same book . . .
More about rain, including experiments and interesting facts.

Books for a Rainy Day

Cloudy with a Chance of Meatballs
by Judi Barrett
It's raining, it's pouring — maple syrup? This town sure has some unusual weather.

Weather
by Seymour Simon
Do all clouds seem to look the same to you? Learn how to identify them.

Come a Tide
by George Ella Lyon
For four days and nights, rain has been falling like a curtain.

Hurricanes and Tornadoes
by Norman S. Barrett
Get the facts on what causes stormy weather.

The Story of Lightning and Thunder
by Ashley Bryan
Long ago, Lightning and Thunder lived on the earth and caused a lot of trouble.

About the Author
Franklyn M. Branley

Franklyn Branley was a fourth grade teacher for many years and has written more than 100 books about scientific topics from comets to earthquakes. He was also an astronomer at the American Museum-Hayden Planetarium in New York City.

Meet the Illustrator
George Guzzi

Space and flying are two of George Guzzi's main interests. He is a member of the NASA Art Program and has been lucky enough to see four space shuttle launches at Cape Canaveral in Florida.

Tornado Alert

by Franklyn M. Branley

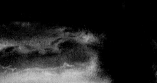

Tornadoes are powerful storms.

On a tornado day the air is hot and still. Clouds build up rapidly. They get thick and dark. In the distance there is thunder and lightning, rain and hail.

Here and there parts of the clouds seem to reach toward the ground. Should these parts grow larger and become funnel shaped, watch out. The funnels could become tornadoes.

The funnel of a tornado is usually dark gray or black. It may also be yellowish or red.

The colors come from red and yellow dirt picked up by the tornado as it moves along the ground.

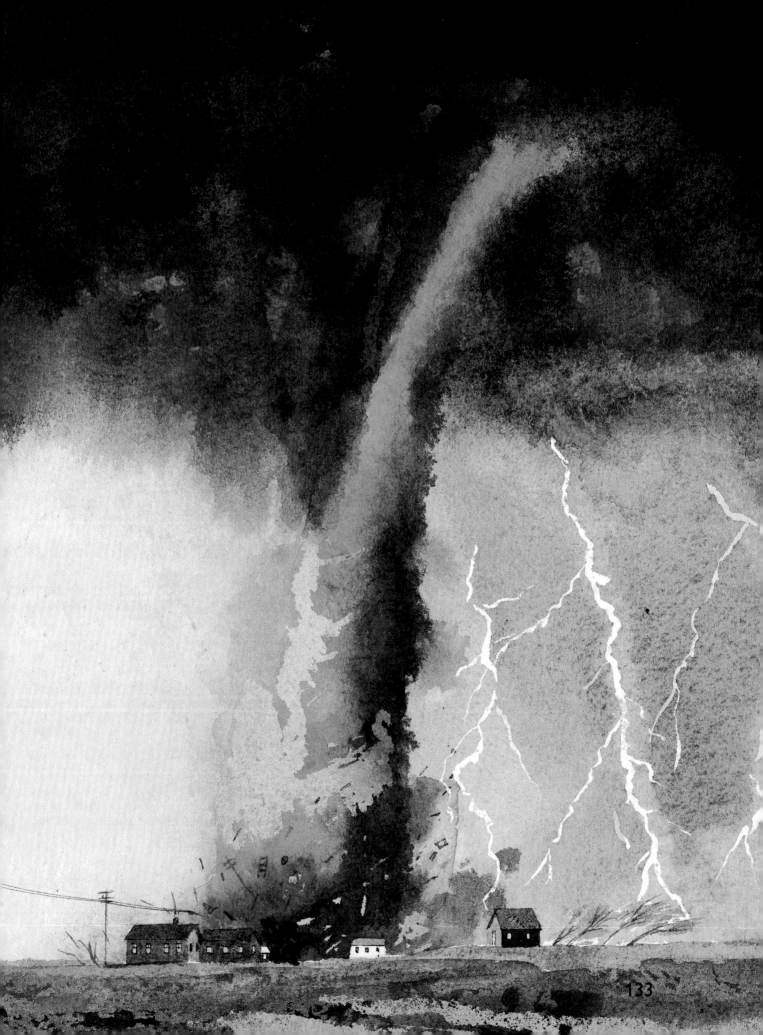

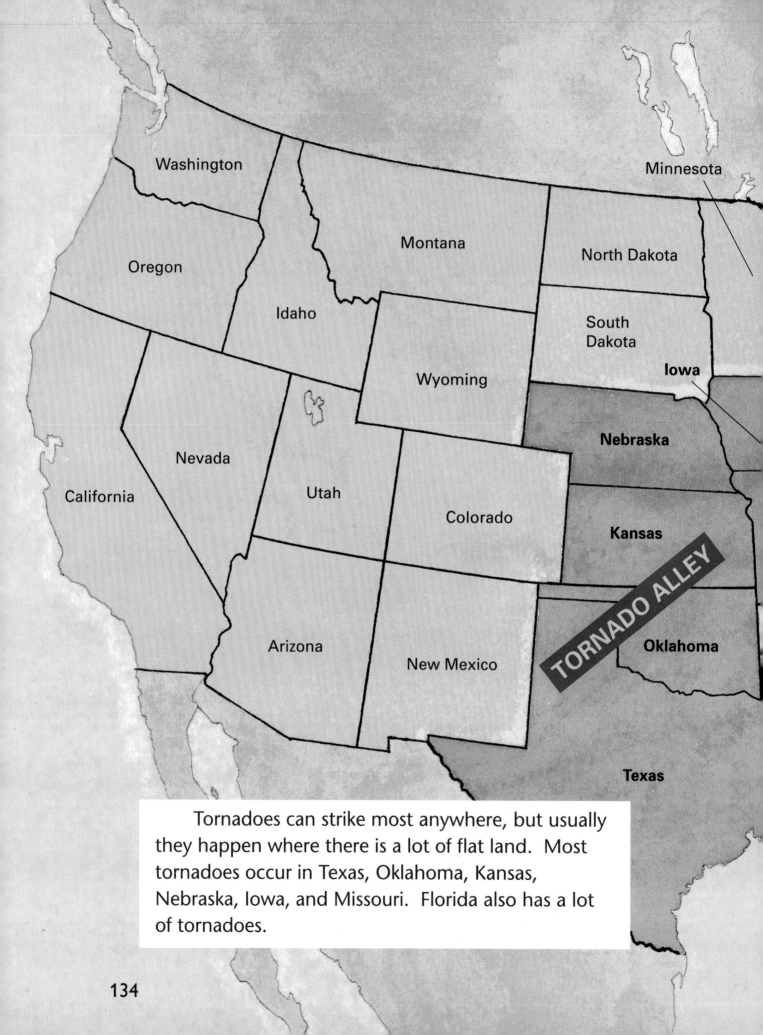

Washington

Minnesota

Montana

North Dakota

Oregon

Idaho

South Dakota

Wyoming

Iowa

Nevada

Nebraska

California

Utah

Colorado

Kansas

TORNADO ALLEY

Arizona

New Mexico

Oklahoma

Texas

Tornadoes can strike most anywhere, but usually they happen where there is a lot of flat land. Most tornadoes occur in Texas, Oklahoma, Kansas, Nebraska, Iowa, and Missouri. Florida also has a lot of tornadoes.

Wisconsin

Michigan

New York

Vermont

Maine

New Hampshire

Massachusetts

Rhode Island

Connecticut

Pennsylvania

New Jersey

Maryland

Delaware

Illinois

Indiana

Ohio

West Virginia

Virginia

Kentucky

Missouri

North Carolina

Tennessee

Arkansas

South Carolina

Alabama

Georgia

Mississippi

Florida

Louisiana

Tornadoes can touch down over seas and lakes. When that happens, they are called waterspouts.

Most tornadoes occur during April, May, and June. That's when cold air meets warm air near the Earth's surface. The cold air pushes under the warm air. The warm air is lighter than the cold air and rises rapidly.

As the warm air moves upward, it spins around, or twists. That's why tornadoes are sometimes called twisters. Some people call them cyclones. The wind speed around the funnel of the tornado may reach 300 miles an hour. No other wind on Earth blows that fast.

As the hot air rises, it also spreads out. It makes a funnel of air, with the small part of the funnel touching the ground and the large part in the dark clouds. Air all around the tornado moves in toward the funnel. At the same time, storm winds push the twisting funnel, moving it along the Earth.

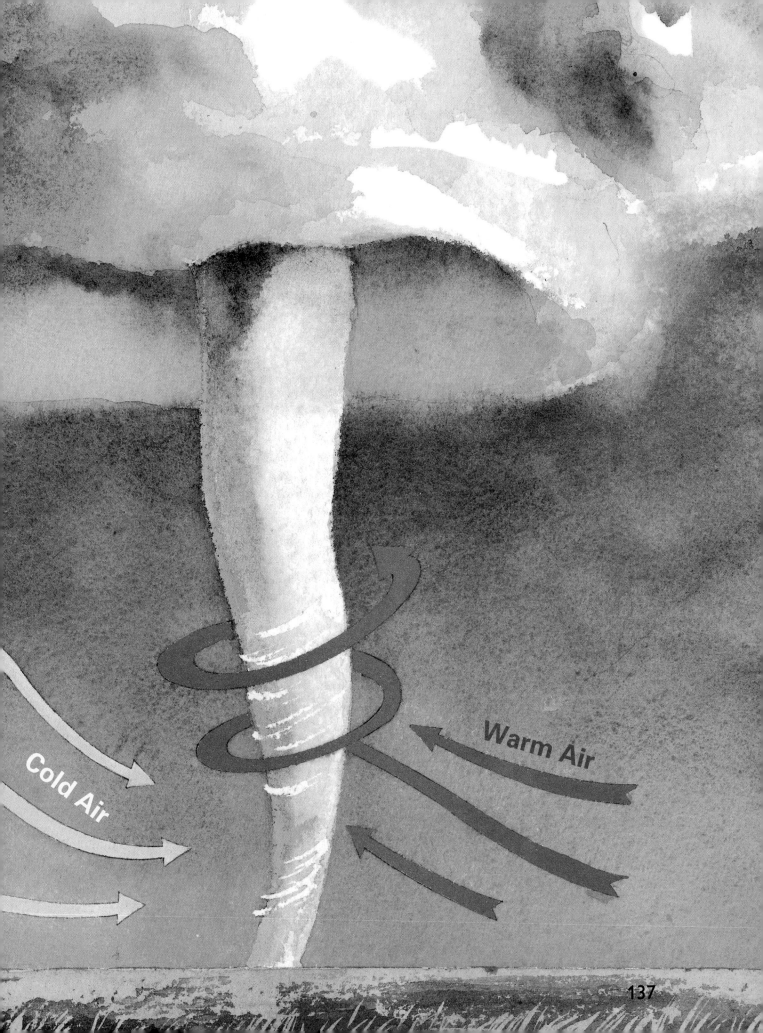

Cold Air

Warm Air

137

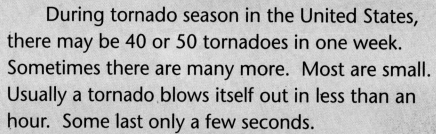

During tornado season in the United States, there may be 40 or 50 tornadoes in one week. Sometimes there are many more. Most are small. Usually a tornado blows itself out in less than an hour. Some last only a few seconds.

Small tornadoes don't travel far, and they cause little damage. Big tornadoes destroy everything in their paths. They may travel two hundred miles and last several hours.

During a tornado there is thunder and lightning, rain and hail. And there is lots of noise. It can sound as loud as a freight train or a jet engine. The word *tornado* comes from a Latin word that means thunder. Some of the noise does come from thunder, but most of it comes from the roaring wind. There is lots of noise, and lots and lots of wind.

Tornadoes are very powerful, and some cause a lot of damage. Tornadoes can pick up branches and boards, stones and bricks, cars, and sometimes even people.

They can rip off roofs and leave a trail of wrecked houses. A tornado's path may be only 20 or 30 feet wide. Or it might be 1000 feet or more — maybe even a mile.

In 1931 a tornado in Minnesota lifted a train off its tracks. The train and its passengers were carried through the air and dropped 80 feet from the tracks. There were 170 people on board. Though many people were hurt, only one person was killed. But in 1974, a series of tornadoes in Missouri, Illinois, Indiana, and ten other states killed 315 people in twenty-four hours.

Scientists keep a close watch during tornado season. They use satellites that see storms developing. And there is radar to detect tornadoes.

Tornado spotters are people who watch for tornadoes. They tell radio and television stations to warn people about tornadoes while the twisters are still far away. The warnings tell people to go to a safe spot, where the tornado can't hurt them.

If a tornado is on its way, here's what you should do. Go to a nearby storm cellar. Storm cellars are underground rooms with heavy doors. They are safe.

If you are in a mobile home, get out of it. A tornado can rip apart a mobile home, even when it is tied down with strong cables. Lie face down in a ditch and cover your head with your hands. When you're in a ditch, sticks and stones flying through the air can't hit you.

If you are in a house, go to the basement and crouch under the stairs or under a heavy workbench. Or go to a closet that is far from an outside wall. Be sure to keep far away from windows. The wind could smash them and send splinters of glass through the air.

If you are in school, follow directions. Your teacher will take you to a basement or to an inside hall. Crouch on your knees near an inner wall. Bend over and clasp your hands behind your head. Most important, keep away from glass windows.

If you are out in the country in a car, don't try to race the tornado. Get out, and find a ditch to lie in.

When there's a tornado, there is also thunder and lightning. So keep away from metal things and from anything that uses electricity. Lightning can travel along metal pipes, and also along electric and telephone wires.

Listen to a battery radio. The radio will tell you when the storm has passed by. Stay where you are safe until you are sure the tornado is over.

Tornadoes are scary. Even if you are not right in the funnel, there is heavy rain all around, dark skies, thunder, lightning, and lots of wind. Often there will be hailstones. They may be as big as golf balls, or even bigger.

Don't panic. Know what to do when there is a tornado. And know where to go.

There is no way to stop tornadoes. But you can be safe from them when you know what to do.

TORNADO RULES

DON'T PANIC
LISTEN
LOOK
FOLLOW DIRECTIONS !

Look What's Coming

Write a Shape Poem

Twisting Words Around

Write a poem in the shape of a tornado. Use storm words from the selection. You might want to collect all the poems into a class book.

Give a Radio Broadcast

We Interrupt This Program . . .

Perform a radio broadcast as if a tornado were on its way to your area. Before you begin, brainstorm a list of safety rules that people need to follow.

On The Air

149

Who Has Seen the Wind?

Who has seen the wind?
  Neither I nor you:
But when the leaves hang trembling,
  The wind is passing through.

Who has seen the wind?
  Neither you nor I:
But when the trees bow down their heads,
  The wind is passing by.

– *Christina Rossetti*

175 SCIENCE EXPERIMENTS TO AMUSE AND AMAZE YOUR FRIENDS

Wind and Weather

by Brenda Walpole

Changes in temperature and pressure make large sections of the air move about. This moving air is called the wind. The direction of the wind and the speed at which it moves affects our weather.

Information about the wind is gathered from weather stations, ships, and satellites out in space. The data is used to predict the weather.

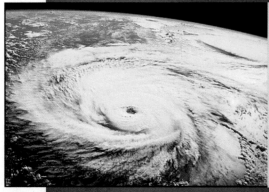

A dramatic view of a typhoon taken from a satellite out in space. Typhoons are violent hurricanes in the China seas. The name "typhoon" may either come from the Chinese words *tai fung* (which mean "wind which strikes") or from the Greek monster Typhoes, who was the father of storm winds.

How Fast Does the Wind Move?

In 1806, an English admiral called Sir Francis Beaufort worked out a scale from 0–12 to indicate the strength of the wind. His scale was based on the effect of the wind on objects such as trees and houses. The speed of the wind was added later. The scale is used today if there are no instruments available to measure wind speed.

The strongest winds on the scale are called hurricanes, typhoons, or cyclones. They travel at more than 95 miles per hour (150 kilometers per hour).

Force: 0
Strength: Calm
Speed: Under 2½ mph
Effect: Smoke goes straight up.

Force: 1–3
Strength: Light breeze
Speed: 2½–15 mph
Effect: Small branches move.

Force: 4–5
Strength: Moderate wind
Speed: 15–29 mph
Effect: Small trees sway a little.

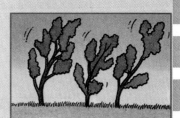

Force: 6–7
Strength: Strong wind
Speed: 30–45 mph
Effect: Big trees sway a little.

Force: 8–9
Strength: Gale
Speed: 45–70 mph
Effect: Slates fall off.

Force: 10–11
Strength: Storm
Speed: 70–95 mph
Effect: Widespread damage.

Force: 12
Strength: Hurricane
Speed: Above 95 mph
Effect: Disaster.

153

Make a
Wind Vane

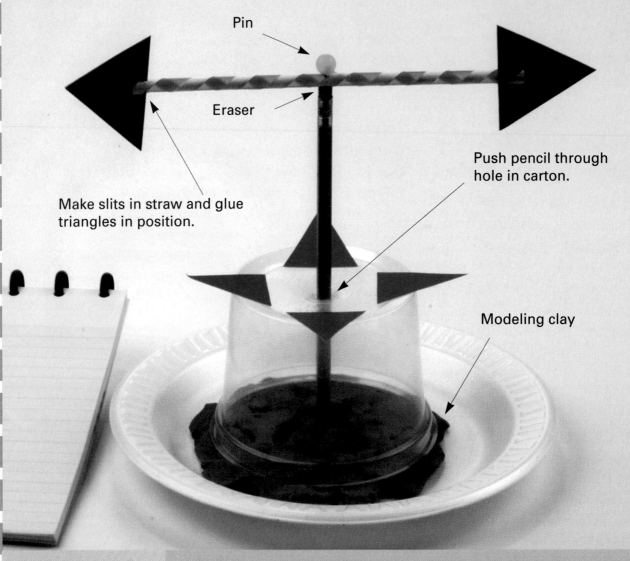

Pin

Eraser

Make slits in straw and glue triangles in position.

Push pencil through hole in carton.

Modeling clay

Equipment

Modeling clay, carton, pencil with eraser, pin, straw, card, glue

Use the information from your wind vane to make a chart showing which direction the wind is blowing from each day. Weather forecasters always talk about the direction that the wind is blowing from. A west wind blows from the west to the east, for example. Does the direction of the wind affect the weather in your area?

1. Make a hole in the middle of the bottom of the carton and push the pencil into the hole.

2. Fix the carton to the thick card with modeling clay.

3. Cut two small triangles of thin card and fix one in each end of the straw.

4. Push the pin through the middle of the straw and into the eraser.

5. Put the wind vane on a flat surface outside. Use a compass to mark north, south, east, and west on the carton. (If you do not have a compass, look at the sun. It rises in the east and sets in the west.)

About the Author
Mary Stolz

Although writing books for children is her favorite pastime, Mary Stolz also likes to read, go bird watching, look at cats, play Scrabble, and cheer for her favorite baseball team, the Atlanta Braves. One of her first jobs was selling books at Macy's department store.

About the Illustrator
Pat Cummings

It's easy for Pat Cummings to lose track of time when she's illustrating a book. She sometimes works all night. Then, as a reward for finishing a page, she goes to the movies. Since there are usually thirty-two pages in a children's book, Cummings sees a lot of movies! Here she's pictured with her cat, Cash, the model for Ringo in *Storm in the Night*.

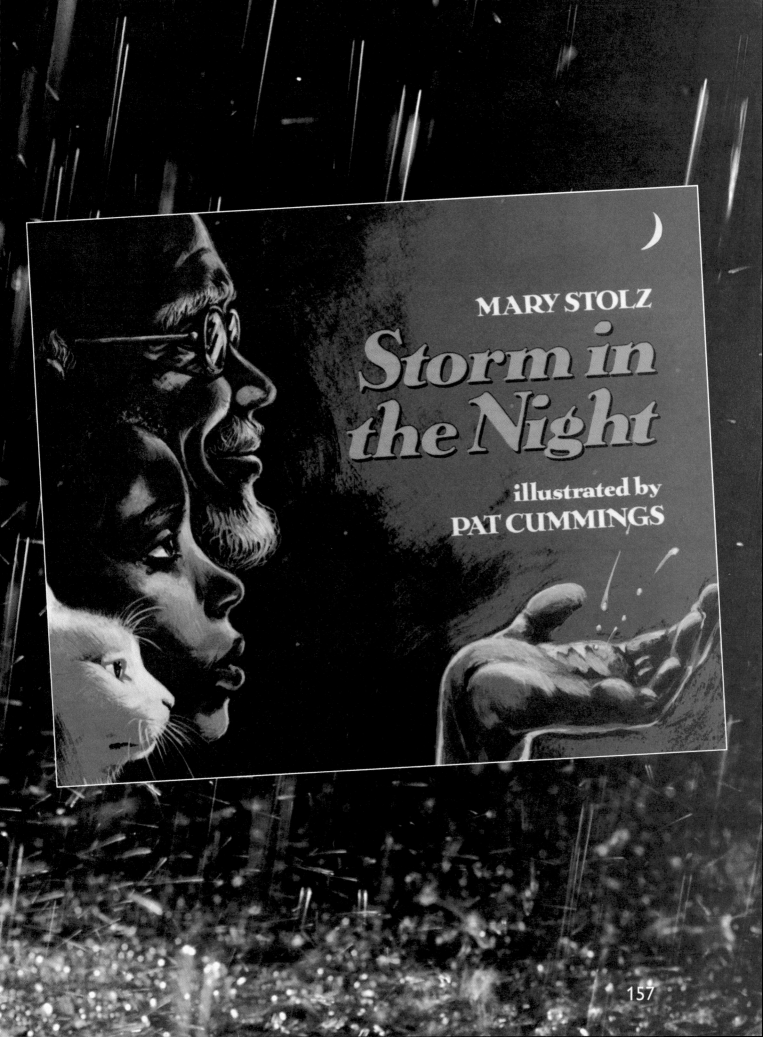

MARY STOLZ

Storm in the Night

illustrated by
PAT CUMMINGS

Storm in the night.

Thunder like mountains blowing up. Lightning licking the navy-blue sky. Rain streaming down the windows, babbling in the downspouts.

And Grandfather? . . . And Thomas? . . . And Ringo, the cat? They were in the dark. Except for Ringo's shining mandarin eyes and the carrot-colored flames in the wood stove, they were quite in the dark.

"We can't read," said Grandfather.

"We can't look at TV," said Thomas.

"Too early to go to bed," said Grandfather.

Thomas sighed. "What will we do?"

"No help for it," said Grandfather, "I shall have to tell you a tale of when I was a boy."

Thomas smiled in the shadows. It was not easy to believe that Grandfather had once been a boy, but Thomas believed it. Because Grandfather said so, Thomas believed that long, long ago, probably at the beginning of the world, his grandfather had been a boy. As Thomas was a boy now, and always would be. A grandfather could be a boy, if he went back in his memory far enough; but a boy could not be a grandfather.

Ringo could not grow up to be a kangaroo, and a boy could not grow up to be an old man. And that, said Thomas to himself, is that.

Grandfather was big and bearded. Thomas had a chin as smooth as a peach. Grandfather had a voice like a tuba. Thomas's voice was like a penny whistle.

"I'm thinking," said Thomas.

"Ah," said Grandfather.

"I'm trying to think what you were like when you were my age."

"That's what I was like," said Grandfather.

"What?"

"Like someone your age."

"Did you look like me?"

"Very much like you."

"But you didn't have a beard."

"Not a sign of one."

"You were short, probably."

"Short, certainly."

"And your voice. It was like mine?"

"Exactly."

Thomas sighed. He just could not imagine it. He stopped trying.

He tried instead to decide whether to ask for a new story or an old one. Grandfather knew more stories than a book full of stories. Thomas hadn't heard all of them yet, because he kept asking for repeats. As he thought about what to ask for, he listened to the sounds of the dark. Grandfather listened too.

In the house a door creaked. A faucet leaked. Ringo scratched on his post, then on Grandfather's chair. He scratched behind his ear, and they could hear even that. In the stove the flames made a fluttering noise.

"That's funny," said Thomas. "I can hear better in the dark than I can when the lights are on."

"No doubt because you are just listening," said his grandfather, "and not trying to see and hear at the same time."

That made sense to Thomas, and he went on listening for sounds in the dark.

There were the clocks. The chiming clock on the mantel struck the hour of eight. *Ping, ping, ping, ping, ping, ping, ping,*

ping-a-ling. The kitchen clock, very excited. *Tickticktickticktick**tickety**.*

There were outside sounds for the listening, too. The bells in the Congregational church rang through the rain. *Bong, bong, bong, bong, bong, bong, bong, BONG!*

Automobile tires swished on the rain-wet streets. Horns honked and hollered. A siren whined in the distance.

"Grandfather," said Thomas, "were there automobiles when you were a boy?"

"Were there *automobiles!*" Grandfather shouted. "How old do you think I am?"

"Well . . ." said Thomas.

"Next thing, you'll be asking if there was electricity when I was your age."

"Oh, Grandfather!" said Thomas, laughing. After a while he said, "Was there?"

"Let's go out on the porch," said Grandfather. "There's too much silliness in here."

By the light of the lightning they made their way to the front door and out on the porch. Ringo, who always followed Thomas, followed him and jumped to the railing.

The rain, driving hard against the back of the house, was scarcely sprinkling here. But it whooped windily through the great beech tree on the lawn, brandishing branches, tearing off twigs. It drenched the bushes, splashed in the birdbath, clattered on the tin roof like a million tacks.

Grandfather and Thomas sat on the swing, creaking back and forth, back and forth, as thunder boomed and lightning stabbed across the sky. Ringo's fur rose, and he turned his head from side to side, his eyes wide and wild in the flashes that lit up the night.

The air smelled peppery and gardeny and new. "That's funny," said Thomas. "I can smell better in the dark, too."

Thomas thought Grandfather answered, but he couldn't hear, as just then a bolt of lightning cracked into the big beech tree. It ripped off a mighty bough, which crashed to the ground.

This was too much for Ringo. He leaped onto Thomas's lap and shivered there. "Poor boy," said Thomas. "He's frightened."

"I had a dog when I was a boy," said Grandfather. "He was so scared of storms that I had to hide under the bed with him when one came. He was afraid even to be frightened alone."

"*I'm* not afraid of *anything*," Thomas said, holding his cat close.

"Not many people can say that," said Grandfather. Then he added, "Well, I suppose anybody could *say* it."

171

"I'm not afraid of thunderstorms, like Ringo and your dog. What was his name?"

"Melvin."

"That's not a good name for a dog," Thomas said.

"I thought it was," Grandfather said calmly. "He was my dog."

"I like cats," said Thomas. "I want to own a *tiger*!"

"Not while you're living with me," said Grandfather.

"Okay," Thomas said. "Is there a story about Melvin?"

"There is. One very good one."

"Tell it," Thomas commanded. "Please, I mean."

"Well," said Grandfather, "when Melvin and I were pups together, I was just as afraid of storms as he was."

"No!" said Thomas.

"Yes," said Grandfather. "We can't all be brave as tigers."

"I guess not," Thomas agreed.

"So there we were, the two of us, hiding under beds whenever a storm came."

"Think of that . . ." said Thomas.

"That's what I'm doing," said Grandfather. "Anyway, the day came when Melvin was out on some errand of his own, and I was doing my homework, when all at once, with only a rumble of warning . . . *down* came the rain, *down* came the lightning, and all around and everywhere came the thunder."

"Wow," said Thomas. "What did you do?"

"Dove under the bed."

"But what about Melvin?"

"I'm *coming* to that," said Grandfather. "What-about-Melvin is what the story is *about*."

"I see," said Thomas. "This is pretty exciting."

"Well — it was then. Are you going to listen, or keep interrupting?"

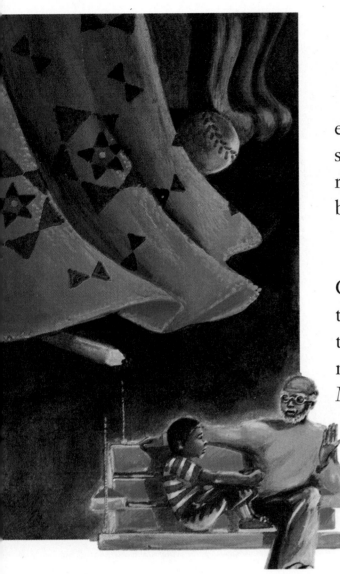

"I think I'll listen," said Thomas.

"Good. Where was I?"

"Under the bed."

"So I was. Well, I lay there shivering at every clap of thunder, and I'm ashamed to say that it was some time before I even remembered that my poor little dog was all by himself out in the storm."

Thomas shook his head in the dark.

"And when I did remember," Grandfather went on, "I had the most awful time making myself wriggle out from under the bed and go looking for my father or my mother — to ask them to go out and find Melvin for me."

"Grandfather!"

"I told you I was afraid. This is a true story you're hearing, so I have to tell the truth."

"Of course," said Thomas, admiring his grandfather for telling a truth like *that*. "Did you find them?"

"I did not. They had gone out someplace for an hour or so, but I'd forgotten. Thomas, fear does strange things to people . . . makes them forget everything but how afraid they are. You wouldn't know about that, of course."

Thomas stroked his cat and said nothing.

"In any case," Grandfather went on, "there I was, alone and afraid in the kitchen, and there was my poor little dog alone and afraid in the storm."

"What did you *do*?" Thomas demanded. "You didn't *leave* him out there, did you Grandfather?"

"Thomas — I put on my raincoat and opened the kitchen door and stepped out on the back porch just as a flash of lightning shook the whole sky and a clap of thunder barreled down and a huge

man *appeared* out of the darkness, holding Melvin in his arms!"

"Whew!"

"That man was seven feet tall and had a face like a crack in the ice."

"Grandfather! You said you were telling me a true story."

"It's true, because that's how he looked to me. He stood there, scowling at me, and said, 'Son, is this your dog?' and I nodded, because I was too scared to speak. 'If you don't take better care of him, you shouldn't have him at all,' said the terrible man. He pushed Melvin at me and stormed off into the dark."

"Gee," said Thomas. "That wasn't very fair. He didn't know you were frightened too. I mean, Grandfather, how old were you?"

"Just about your age."

"Well, some people my age can get pretty frightened."

"Not you, of course."

Thomas said nothing.

"Later on," Grandfather continued, "I realized that man wasn't seven feet tall, or even terrible. He was worried about the puppy, so he didn't stop to think about me."

"Well, *I* think he should have."

"People don't always do what they should, Thomas."

"What's the end of the story?"

"Oh, just what you'd imagine," Grandfather said carelessly. "Having overcome my fear enough to forget myself and think about Melvin, I wasn't afraid of storms anymore."

"Oh, good," said Thomas.

For a while they were silent. The storm was spent. There were only flickers of lightning, mutterings of thunder, and a little patter of rain.

"When are the lights going to come on?" Thomas asked.

"You know as much as I do," said Grandfather.

"Maybe they won't come on for hours," said Thomas. "Maybe they won't come on until *tomorrow*!"

"Maybe not."

"Maybe they'll *never* come on again, and what will we do then?"

"We'll think of something," said Grandfather.

"Grandfather?"

"Yes, Thomas?"

"What I think . . . I think that maybe if you hadn't been here, and Ringo hadn't been here, and I was all alone in the house and there was a storm and the lights went out and didn't come on again for a long time, like this . . . I think maybe *then* I would be a *little* bit afraid."

"Perfectly natural," said Grandfather.

Thomas sighed. Grandfather yawned. Ringo jumped to the porch floor and walked daintily into the garden, shaking his legs.

After a while the lights came on.

They turned them off and went to bed.

After the Storm

Make a Guidebook

Rain, Rain, Go Away

It's raining outside and you're stuck inside. What can you do? Work with a classmate to make a guidebook of suggestions for things to do on a rainy day.

Perform Reader's Theater

Ping, Ping, Ping-a-ling

With a group, read aloud a scene from the story. Two classmates can read the parts of Thomas and Grandfather, while others can make sound effects for all the sounds in the night.

Snowy Winter Days

A Description by Annie Holstein

Do you have **snowy days where you live?** Annie's description can help you imagine a snowy day even if you live in a warm place.

Snowy Winter Days

I love snowy winter days.
Sometimes during the night the
snow floats down quietly like the sound
of a butterfly kiss. Then, in the dark early
morning, I hear snow shovels scrape against
the stones on the driveway. That's how I
know my parents are going to work. The
heavy red snow plows snarl and grumble as
they clear our hilly street. Whrrr –
the cars slip and slide trying to climb
the slippery hill.

The snow smells cold and fresh.
When school is closed for a snow day,

our house smells like the cookies
we bake after we come inside.

Zoom! My sled flies down the
hill. Snow shoots into my face like
tingly little beads. Snowflakes melt in
my mouth. They make a watery pool on
my tongue. When I eat the snow, it
tastes like ice.

I love most the way the snow
looks like milk-white crystals poured
out of the clouds. In the sunlight the
snow glitters gold. At night it
glitters silver.

Annie Holstein
Underwood Elementary School
Newton, Massachusetts

When Annie wrote this description in third
grade, she said, "I started with a list of the
different senses, and I tried to describe each
one. The taste and sound of snow were hard."
Annie enjoys swimming, gymnastics,
ballet, and playing the piano. She would like
to be an archaeologist.

The Greatest Storms on Earth

Streaks of electricity hotter than the surface of the sun flash across the sky. A tornado picks up a house and drops it hundreds of feet away. A wall of water 25 feet high rushes to shore, pushed by 200 m.p.h. hurricane winds. The surprising thing is, events like these are common. Every year, storms kill and injure thousands of people around the world and cause billions of dollars worth of damage. All we can do in the face of their might is take cover and wait for the storm to pass.

Thunderstorms & Lightning

▲ It's estimated that lightning strikes the U.S. 40 million times each year.
- A lightning bolt lasts only 1/10 of a second, but it has enough power — 30 million volts — to light up all New York City.
- An average thunderstorm is more powerful than an atomic bomb.

- Lightning ignites about half of U.S. forest fires.
- Lightning streaks across the sky in a path several inches across, heating the air around it to 20,000 degrees Fahrenheit or hotter. The heat causes the air to expand violently, creating the explosion we hear as thunder.

▲ To gauge how many miles you are from a thunderstorm, as soon as you see lightning, count the seconds until you hear thunder. Then divide the total by five.

▼ To prove that lightning is electricity, Benjamin Franklin flew a kite in a thunderstorm (a very dangerous thing to do!). A spark jumped from a key on the tail of the kite to his hand. Franklin also invented the lightning rod, a device that is put atop houses to deflect lightning.

Tornadoes

WARNING!

Go to a cellar when a tornado is approaching. If you don't have one, go into a closet as far away from the outside walls of your house as possible.

▲ Tornadoes are by far the most destructive storms on earth. Winds in the whirling black column called a funnel cloud can exceed 300 m.p.h. The funnel cloud is like a giant vacuum cleaner, picking up cars, houses, and everything else in its path.

After a tornado has passed, people notice some strange things. Sometimes, for instance, pieces of wheat are rammed through trees like arrows, or a school of fish ends up in someone's front yard.

About 75 percent of all tornadoes occur in the U.S.

▲ Dust devils are funnels of hot air that whirl up from the desert and other dry, dusty places.

Hurricanes
WARNING!

In many coastal areas, the only safe bet when a hurricane is approaching is to get into a car and head inland.

TAXI

TULSA, OKLAHOMA! AND STEP ON IT!

▲ As the air soaks up warm moisture from the sea, thunderclouds begin to form. Strong winds in the atmosphere cause these clouds to swirl.

As a storm continues to move over warm water, it gets bigger and bigger and the winds become more violent.

A hurricane is in full force when a center of calm, the eye, forms inside the swirling winds. The strongest winds, up to 225 m.p.h., are found just outside the eye, but it can be very windy and rainy as far as 250 miles away from the eye.

◄ 40 million Americans live in coastal areas that are vulnerable to hurricanes. In 1992, Hurricane Andrew wreaked havoc in southern Florida and Louisiana.

▼ Scientists use photos taken by satellite to track hurricanes as they form over the oceans.

▼ The eye of a hurricane is the center of the storm, where winds usually don't exceed 15 m.p.h. Planes can fly into it to take measurements.

HURRICANE ANDREW
8/24/92 AT 2030Z

GOES-7 VIS

SIMULATED GOES-I VIS

Other Wild Weather

Aside from mighty storms, weather shows its fury in other ways, too.

▼ When it doesn't rain enough, there's drought. In the 1930s, a seven-year-long drought turned 50 million acres of Midwest farmland into the devastating Dust Bowl.

▼ For six months out of the year in India, it doesn't rain, it pours. Monsoons drop hundreds of inches of rain, sometimes as much as a foot a day.

Meet William Steig

William Steig began his career as a cartoonist. At the age of sixty-one, he wrote and illustrated his first children's book, *Roland the Minstrel Pig*. Over the next fifteen years, Steig wrote and illustrated more than a dozen books, such as *Sylvester and the Magic Pebble* and *Doctor De Soto*. All of them featured animals as the main characters. *Brave Irene* is his first book with a person as the main character.

Brave Irene

by William Steig

Mrs. Bobbin, the dressmaker, was tired and had a bad headache, but she still managed to sew the last stitches in the gown she was making.

"It's the most beautiful dress in the whole world!" said her daughter, Irene. "The duchess will love it."

"It *is* nice," her mother admitted. "But, dumpling, it's for tonight's ball, and I don't have the strength to bring it. I feel sick."

"Poor Mama," said Irene. "I can get it there!"

"No, cupcake, I can't let you," said Mrs. Bobbin. "Such a huge package, and it's such a long way to the palace. Besides, it's starting to snow."

"But I *love* snow," Irene insisted. She coaxed her mother into bed, covered her with two quilts, and added a blanket for her feet. Then she fixed her some tea with lemon and honey and put more wood in the stove.

With great care, Irene took the splendid gown down from the dummy and packed it in a big box with plenty of tissue paper.

"Dress warmly, pudding," her mother called in a weak voice, "and don't forget to button up. It's cold out there, and windy."

Irene put on her fleece-lined boots, her red hat and muffler, her heavy coat, and her mittens. She kissed her mother's hot forehead six times, then once again, made sure she was tucked in snugly, and slipped out with the big box, shutting the door firmly behind her.

It really was cold outside, very cold. The wind
whirled the falling snowflakes about, this way, that way,
and into Irene's squinting face. She set out on the uphill
path to Farmer Bennett's sheep pasture.

By the time she got there, the snow was up to her
ankles and the wind was worse. It hurried her along and
made her stumble. Irene resented this; the box was

problem enough. "Easy does it!" she cautioned the wind, leaning back hard against it.

By the middle of the pasture, the flakes were falling thicker. Now the wind drove Irene along so rudely she had to hop, skip, and go helter-skeltering over the knobby ground. Cold snow sifted into her boots and chilled her feet. She pushed out her lip and hurried on. This was an important errand.

When she reached Apple Road, the wind decided to put on a show. It ripped branches from trees and flung them about, swept up and scattered the fallen snow, got in front of Irene to keep her from moving ahead. Irene turned around and pressed on backwards.

"Go home!" the wind squalled. "Irene . . . go hooooooome . . ."

"I will do no such thing," she snapped. "No such thing, you wicked wind!"

"Go ho–o–ome," the wind yodeled. "GO HO —
WO — WOME," it shrieked, "or else." For a short
second, Irene wondered if she shouldn't heed the wind's
warning. But no! *The gown had to get to the duchess!*

The wind wrestled her for the package — walloped
it, twisted it, shook it, snatched at it. But Irene wouldn't
yield. "It's my mother's work!" she screamed.

Then — oh, woe! — the box was wrenched from
her mittened grasp and sent bumbling along in the snow.
Irene went after it.

201

She pounced and took hold, but the ill-tempered
wind ripped the box open. The ball gown flounced
out and went waltzing through the powdered air with
tissue-paper attendants.

Irene clung to the empty box and watched the
beautiful gown disappear.

How could anything so terribly wrong be allowed
to happen? Tears froze on her lashes. Her dear
mother's hard work, all those days of measuring, cutting,
pinning, stitching . . . for *this?* And the poor duchess!
Irene decided she would have to trudge on with just the
box and explain everything in person.

She went shuffling through the snow. Would her mother understand, she wondered, that it was the wind's fault, not hers? Would the duchess be angry? The wind was howling like a wild animal.

Suddenly Irene stepped in a hole and fell over with a twisted ankle. She blamed it on the wind. "Keep quiet!" she scolded. "You've done enough damage already. You've spoiled everything! *Everything!*" The wind swallowed up her words.

She sat in the snow in great pain, afraid she wouldn't be able to go on. But she managed to get to her feet and start moving. It hurt. Home, where she longed to be, where she and her mother could be warm together, was far behind. It's got to be closer to the palace, she thought. But where any place was in all this snow, she couldn't be sure.

She plowed on, dragging furrows with her sore foot. The short winter day was almost done.

Am I still going the right way, she wondered. There was no one around to advise her. Whoever else there was in this snow-covered world was far, far away, and safe indoors — even the animals in their burrows. She went plodding on.

Soon night took over. She knew in the dark that the muffled snow was still falling — she could feel it. She was cold and alone in the middle of nowhere. Irene was lost.

She had to keep moving. She was hoping she'd
come to a house, any house at all, and be taken in. She
badly needed to be in someone's arms. The snow was
above her knees now. She shoved her way through it,
clutching the empty box.

She was asking how long a small person could
keep this struggle up, when she realized it was getting
lighter. There was a soft glow coming from somewhere
below her.

She waded toward this glow, and soon was gazing
down a long slope at a brightly lit mansion. It had to be
the palace!

207

Irene pushed forward with all her strength and —
sloosh! thwump! — she plunged downward and was
buried. She had fallen off a little cliff. Only her hat
and the box in her hands stuck out above the snow.

Even if she could call for help, no one would hear
her. Her body shook. Her teeth chattered. Why not
freeze to death, she thought, and let all these troubles
end. Why not? She was already buried.

And never see her mother's face again? Her good mother who smelled like fresh-baked bread? In an explosion of fury, she flung her body about to free herself and was finally able to climb up on her knees and look around.

How to get down to that glittering palace? As soon as she raised the question, she had the answer.

She laid the box down and climbed aboard. But it pressed into the snow and stuck. She tried again, and this time, instead of climbing on, she leaped. The box shot forward, like a sled.

The wind raced after Irene but couldn't keep up. In a moment she would be with people again, inside where it was warm. The sled slowed and jerked to a stop on paving stones.

The time had come to break the bad news to the duchess. With the empty box clasped to her chest, Irene strode nervously toward the palace.

But then her feet stopped moving and her mouth fell open. She stared. Maybe this was impossible, yet there it was, a little way off and over to the right, hugging the trunk of a tree — the beautiful ball gown! The wind was holding it there.

"Mama!" Irene shouted. "Mama, I found it!"

She managed somehow, despite the wind's meddling, to get the gown off the tree and back in its box. And in another moment she was at the door of the palace. She knocked twice with the big brass knocker. The door opened and she burst in.

She was welcomed by cheering servants and a
delirious duchess. They couldn't believe she had come
over the mountain in such a storm, all by herself. She
had to tell the whole story, every detail. And she did.

Then she asked to be taken right back to her sick
mother. But it was out of the question, they said; the
road that ran around the mountain wouldn't be cleared
till morning.

"Don't fret, child," said the duchess. "Your mother is surely sleeping now. We'll get you there first thing tomorrow."

Irene was given a good dinner as she sat by the fire, the moisture steaming off her clothes. The duchess, meanwhile, got into her freshly ironed gown before the guests began arriving in their sleighs.

What a wonderful ball it was! The duchess in her
new gown was like a bright star in the sky. Irene in
her ordinary dress was radiant. She was swept up into

dances by handsome aristocrats, who kept her feet off
the floor to spare her ankle. Her mother would enjoy
hearing all about it.

Early the next morning, when snow had long since ceased falling, Mrs. Bobbin woke from a good night's sleep feeling much improved. She hurried about and got a fire going in the cold stove. Then she went to look in on Irene.

But Irene's bed was empty! She ran to the window and gazed at the white landscape. No one out there. Snow powder fell from the branch of a tree.

"Where is my child?" Mrs. Bobbin cried. She whipped on her coat to go out and find her.

When she pulled the door open, a wall of drift faced her. But peering over it, she could see a horse-drawn sleigh hastening up the path. And seated on the sleigh, between two large footmen, was Irene herself, asleep but smiling.

Would you like to hear the rest?

Well, there was a bearded doctor in the back of the sleigh. And the duchess had sent Irene's mother a ginger cake with white icing, some oranges and a pineapple, and spice candy of many flavors, along with a note saying how much she cherished her gown, and what a brave and loving person Irene was.

Which, of course, Mrs. Bobbin knew. Better than the duchess.

Come in from the Cold

Write a Song

The Ballad of Brave Irene

Work with a partner to write and perform a song about Brave Irene. Include details about some of her most difficult moments. You might want to use a tune you already know.

Make a Diorama

What's in the Box?

The trip from Irene's house to the palace was a long one. Make a diorama that shows one of Irene's many adventures along the way. Use a shoebox, cotton balls, and other art supplies.

How Snowmaker was taught a lesson

written and illustrated by C. J. Taylor

How we saw the world

C.J. Taylor

Nine Native stories of the way things began

One winter long ago Snowmaker came down from the North and would not leave. Spring did not come. The birds did not return. Animals hid to escape the bitterly cold winds. Snow covered the ground and ice covered the rivers, making it hard to get food. When the people went to gather firewood Snowmaker stung their ears and noses with the cold. The people feared there would be no spring, summer and autumn and that they would not be able to hunt or fish or find berries.

It was June that year before Snowmaker decided to return to his northern home and the snow started to melt. Gray Wolf called the people together. "We must teach Snowmaker a lesson. He has grown too powerful." He carved a bowl from a large log, put the last of the melting snow into it and placed the bowl in the rays of the sun. As it melted he cried out: "Snowmaker, I am not afraid of you!"

At that moment, as if to warn him, a cold wind blew in from the North. The people were frightened. "Do not anger Snowmaker," they told Gray Wolf, "or next winter will be longer and colder still."

But Gray Wolf was determined to find a way to help his people. He knew that Snowmaker was angry now and would come after him in the autumn. He worked hard all summer. He built a shelter away from the village and piled firewood around it until the shelter was hidden. He kept the furs of the animals he hunted and preserved the meat for food. And he did something different: instead of eating the animal fat as his people normally did, he melted it into oil and kept it in his wooden bowl.

The days grew shorter and autumn came. Cool days were followed by colder nights. One day the sun didn't come out at all. Gray Wolf knew Snowmaker was about to attack. He went into his shelter, pulled his fur robes tightly around him, built a fire and waited for Snowmaker.

Snowmaker came upon the village in a fury. For days he blew his icy breath everywhere and covered the ground with snow as he searched for his enemy. Gray Wolf huddled in his shelter and felt weak from the cold. The wind came through the cracks and made it difficult for him to keep his fire alive. "I have never been this cold," he thought.

Snowmaker found Gray Wolf's shelter and entered it with a blast of cold air. The fire flickered as if about to go out. Snowmaker laughed. "You think you can defeat me?" he sneered.

With the last of his strength Gray Wolf reached for his wooden bowl and threw the oil onto the embers. The flames leaped up and danced around wildly, lighting the shelter. Snowmaker fell back, sweating, panting. "Your fire is too hot for me," Snowmaker cried, cowering in a corner. "You have defeated me," he hissed. "But I will return." With that, he ran from the lodge, leaving a trail of melted snow in his wake. Gray Wolf felt his strength and the warmth outside return.

The people could not believe that Gray Wolf had defeated Snowmaker, not until spring arrived on time that year. Then the hunters learned from Gray Wolf to keep the oils from the animals they brought home so as to make their winter fires burn brightly.

Snowmaker still returns every year with his cold wind, ice and snow. But because of Gray Wolf, Snowmaker is no longer as powerful as he used to be.

Snowflakes

Snow
Snow
Snow
Let me catch you in my mouth!

Ah
Ah
Ah
The flakes keep landing on my nose!

Ha
Ha
Ha
That's my nose, not my mouth!

Suk-Joong Yoon

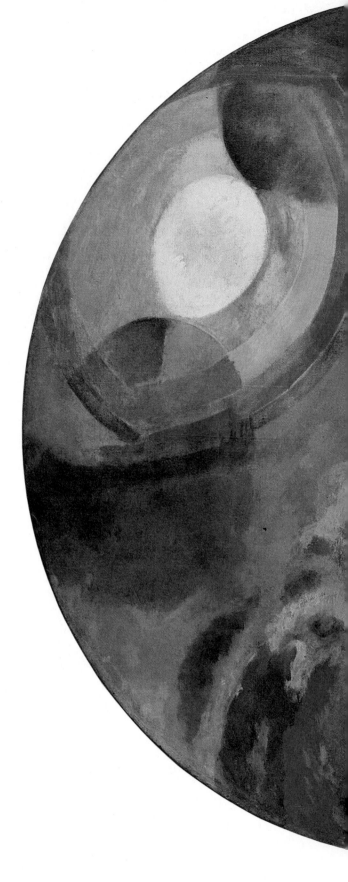

224

Simultaneous Contrasts: Sun and Moon
Robert Delaunay, 1913
    Oil on canvas

Sunflakes

If sunlight fell like snowflakes,
gleaming yellow and so bright,
we could build a sunman,
we could have a sunball fight,
we could watch the sunflakes
drifting in the sky.
We could go sleighing
in the middle of July
through sundrifts and sunbanks,
we could ride a sunmobile,
and we could touch sunflakes —
I wonder how they'd feel.

Frank Asch

225

WHAT A DAY!

Contents

Read On Your Own

PAPERBACK PLUS

Will and Orv

by Walter A. Schulz
Johnny will never forget the day he
saw two brothers' dream take flight.

In the same book . . .
More about the Wright Brothers
and their incredible flying machine.

by Walter A. Schulz
illustrations by Janet Schulz

KALB   The Goof That Won the Pennant

Julian's worried. Dad's dream birthday present is turning into a nightmare!

Julian, Dream Doctor

By Ann Cameron
Illustrated by Ann Strugnell

PAPERBACK **PLUS**

Julian, Dream Doctor

by Ann Cameron
Dad's birthday is coming up, and Julian wants to get him something he's always dreamed of.

In the same book . . .

Fun information about dreams, snakes, and more.

Books to Spend the Day With

Tuesday

by David Wiesner
It's Tuesday evening in the swamp. Suddenly, frogs on their lily pads start soaring through the air.

Saturday at the New You

by Barbara E. Barber
Saturday is Shauna's favorite day — it's the day she helps out at her mother's beauty parlor.

Sara Morton's Day: A Day in the Life of a Pilgrim Girl

by Kate Waters
What was life like for children more than 350 years ago?

Alexander and the Terrible, Horrible, No Good, Very Bad Day

by Judith Viorst
Alexander wakes up to find gum in his hair and no prize in his cereal. And the day has just begun.

BEVERLY CLEARY

RAMONA
AND HER
MOTHER

illustrated by Alan Tiegreen

The Great
Hair Argument

"Ramona, stand on both feet and hold still," said Mrs. Quimby one Saturday morning. "I can't cut your bangs straight when you wiggle."

"I'm trying," said Ramona. Bits of falling hair made her nose tickle. She blew upward, fanning out her bangs from her forehead, to rid herself of the tickle.

"Now see what you've done." Mrs. Quimby recombed the bangs.

Ramona stood perfectly still in an agony of itching, twitching her nose to get rid of snips of falling hair, until her mother finally said, "There, little rabbit, we're finished." She removed the towel from Ramona's shoulders and shook it over the kitchen wastebasket. Ramona, who liked being called a little rabbit, continued to twitch her nose and think of the warm and cozy picture books about bears and rabbits her mother used to read to her at bedtime before she kissed her good-night. She had loved those books. They made her feel safe. During the daytime she had preferred books about steam shovels, the noisier the better, but at night — bears, nice bears, and bunnies.

"Next!" Mrs. Quimby called out to Beezus, who had just washed her hair. These days Beezus spent a lot of time locked in the bathroom with a bottle of shampoo.

"Beezus, don't keep me waiting," said Mrs. Quimby. "I have a lot to do this morning." The washing machine had broken down, and because no one had been able to stay home during the week to admit a repairman, Mrs. Quimby had to drive to a laundromat with three loads of washing. Repairmen did not work on Saturdays.

"I'm waiting," repeated Mrs. Quimby.

Beezus, rubbing her hair with a towel, appeared in the doorway. "Mother, I don't want you to cut my hair," she announced.

Ramona, about to leave the kitchen, decided to stay. She sensed an interesting argument.

"But Beezus, you're so shaggy," protested Mrs. Quimby. "You look untidy."

"I don't want to look tidy," said Beezus. "I want to look nice."

"You look nice when you're neat." Mrs. Quimby's voice told Ramona her mother's patience was stretched thin. "And don't forget, how you look is not as important as how you behave."

"Mother, you're so old-fashioned," said Beezus.

Mrs. Quimby looked both annoyed and amused. "That's news to me."

Beezus plainly resented her mother's amusement. "Well you *are*."

"All right. I'm old-fashioned," said Mrs. Quimby in a way that told Ramona she did not mean what she was saying. "But what are we going to do about your shaggy hair?"

"I am not a sheep dog," said Beezus. "You make me sound like one."

Mrs. Quimby chose silence while Ramona, fascinated, waited to see what would happen next. Deep down she was pleased, and guilty because she was pleased, that her mother was annoyed with Beezus. At the same time, their disagreement worried her. She wanted her family to be happy.

"I want to get my hair cut in a beauty shop," said Beezus. "Like all the other girls."

"Why Beezus, you know we can't afford a luxury like that," said Mrs. Quimby. "Your hair is sensible and easy to care for."

"I'm practically the only girl in my whole class who gets a home haircut," persisted Beezus, ignoring her mother's little speech.

"Now you're exaggerating." Mrs. Quimby looked tired.

Ramona did not like to see her mother look tired so she tried to help. "Karen in my room at school says her mother cuts her hair and her sister's too, and her sister is in your class."

Beezus turned on her sister. "You keep out of this!"

"Let's not get all worked up," said Mrs. Quimby.

"I'm not worked up," said Beezus. "I just don't want to have a home haircut, and I'm not going to have one."

"Be sensible," said Mrs. Quimby.

Beezus scowled. "I've been good old sensible Beezus all my life, and I'm tired of being sensible." She underlined this announcement by adding, "Ramona can get away with anything, but not me. No. I always have to be good old sensible Beezus."

"That's not so." Ramona was indignant. "I never get away with anything."

After a thoughtful moment, Mrs. Quimby spoke. "So am I tired of being sensible all the time."

Both sisters were surprised, Ramona most of all. Mothers were supposed to be sensible. That was what mothers were for.

Mrs. Quimby continued. "Once in a while I would like to do something that isn't sensible."

"Like what?" asked Beezus.

"Oh — I don't know." Mrs. Quimby looked at the breakfast dishes in the sink and at the rain spattering against the windows. "Sit on a cushion in the sunshine, I guess, and blow the fluff off dandelions."

Beezus looked as if she did not quite believe her mother. "Weeds don't bloom this time of year," she pointed out.

Ramona felt suddenly close to her mother and a little shy. "I would like to sit on a cushion and blow dandelion fluff with you," she confided, thinking what fun it would be, just the two of them, sitting in warm sunshine, blowing on the yellow blossoms, sending dandelion down dancing off into the sunlight. She leaned against her mother, who put her arm around her and gave her a little hug. Ramona twitched her nose with pleasure.

"But Mother," said Beezus, "you always said we shouldn't blow on dandelions because we would scatter seeds and they would get started in the lawn and are hard to dig out."

"I know," admitted Mrs. Quimby, her moment of fantasy at an end. "Very sensible of me."

Beezus was silenced for the time being.

"I like your hair, Mother," said Ramona, and she did. Her mother's short hair was straight, parted on one side and usually tucked behind her left ear. It always smelled good and looked, Ramona felt, the way a mother's hair should look, at least the way her mother's hair should look. "I think your hair looks nice," she said, "and I don't mind when you cut my hair." In the interest of truth she added, "Except when my nose tickles."

Beezus flared up once more. "Well, goody-goody for you, you little twerp," she said, and bounced out of the kitchen. In a moment the door of her room slammed.

Ramona's feelings were hurt. "I'm not a little twerp, am I?" she asked, wondering if her mother agreed.

Mrs. Quimby reached for the broom to sweep bits of hair from the kitchen floor. "Of course not," she said. "I don't bring up my daughters to be twerps."

Ramona twitched her nose like a rabbit.

Afterward neither Mrs. Quimby nor Beezus mentioned hair. Beezus's hair grew shaggier and Ramona decided that if her sister did not look like a sheep dog yet, she soon would. She also sensed that, as much as her mother wanted to say something about Beezus's hair, she was determined not to.

Beezus, on the other hand, looked defiant. She sat at the dinner table with a you-can't-make-me-if-I-don't-want-to look on her face.

Ramona discovered that the tiny part of herself, deep down inside, that had been pleased because her mother was angry with her sister was no longer pleased. Anger over one person's hair was not worth upsetting the family.

"Women," muttered Mr. Quimby every evening at supper. He also remarked, as if he had hair on his mind, that he thought he was getting a little thin on top and maybe he should massage his scalp.

Conversation was strained. Beezus avoided speaking to her mother. Mrs. Quimby tried to look as if nothing had happened. She said calmly, "Beezus, when the shampoo bottle is almost empty, don't forget to add shampoo to the grocery list. We use it, too, you know."

"Yes, Mother," said Beezus.

Ramona felt like yelling, Stop it, both of you! She tried to think of interesting things to talk about at the dinner table to make her family forget about hair.

One evening, to distract her family from hair, Ramona was telling how her teacher had explained that the class should not be afraid of big words because big words were often made up of little words: *dishcloth* meant a cloth for washing dishes and *pancake* meant a cake cooked in a pan.

"But I bake cakes in pans — or used to — and this does not make them pancakes," Mrs. Quimby pointed out. "If I bake an angelfood cake in a pan, it is not a pancake."

"I know," said Ramona. "I don't understand it because *carpet* does not mean a pet that rides in a car. Picky-picky is not a carpet when we take him to the vet." At this example her parents laughed, which pleased Ramona until she noticed that Beezus was neither laughing nor listening.

Beezus took a deep breath. "Mother," she said in a determined way that told Ramona her sister was about to say something her mother might not like. The words came out in a rush. "Some of the girls at school get their hair cut at Robert's School of Hair Design. People who are learning to cut hair do the work, but a teacher watches to see that they do it right. It doesn't cost as much as a regular beauty shop. I've saved my allowance, and there's this lady named Dawna who is really good and can cut hair so it looks like that girl who ice skates on TV. You know, the one with the hair that sort of floats when she twirls around and then falls in place when she stops. Please, Mother, I have enough money saved." When Beezus had finished this speech she sat back in her chair with an anxious, pleading expression on her face.

Mrs. Quimby, who had looked tense when Beezus first began to speak, relaxed. "That seems reasonable. Where is Robert's School of Hair Design?"

"In that new shopping center on the other side of town," Beezus explained. "Please, Mother, I'll do anything you want if you'll let me go."

Ramona did not take this promise seriously.

In the interests of family peace, Mrs. Quimby relented. "All right," she said with a small sigh. "But I'll have to drive you over. If you can hold out until Saturday, we'll go see what Dawna can do about your hair after I drive your father to work."

"Oh, thank you, Mother!" Beezus looked happier than she had since the beginning of the great hair argument.

Ramona was pleased, too, even though she knew she would have to be dragged along. Peace in the family was worth a boring morning.

Saturday turned out to be cold, raw, and wet. Ramona despaired of ever using her roller skates. The

Quimbys hurried through breakfast, stacked the dishes in the sink, piled into the car and drove off, windshield wipers flopping furiously, to deliver Mr. Quimby to the Shop-Rite Market. Ramona, resigned to a tiresome morning, could feel Beezus's excitement and see how tightly she clutched her allowance in the drawstring bag she had crocheted.

When Mr. Quimby had been dropped off at the market, Beezus joined her mother in the front seat. She always gets to sit in the front seat, thought Ramona.

Mrs. Quimby started up the on-ramp to the freeway that cut the city in two. "Beezus, watch for the signs. I have to keep my eyes on my driving," she directed.

Ramona thought, I can read, too, if the words aren't too long.

Mrs. Quimby looked back over her shoulder for a space in which to merge with the heavy morning traffic. A space came down the freeway, and Mrs. Quimby managed to fit the car into it. In no time they were crossing the river, which looked cold and gray between the black girders of the bridge. Green signs spanned the freeway.

"Do I turn left?" asked Mrs. Quimby, uncertain of the way to the shopping center.

"Right," said Beezus.

Mrs. Quimby turned right onto the off-ramp.

"Mother," cried Beezus. "You were supposed to turn left."

"Then why did you tell me to turn right?" Mrs. Quimby sounded angry.

"You asked if you should turn left," said Beezus, "and I meant, 'Right, you should turn left.'"

"After this, use your head," said Mrs. Quimby. "Now how do I get back on the freeway?" She drove through a maze of unfamiliar one-way streets looking for an on-ramp sign. Finally she asked for directions from a man at a service station. He looked disagreeable because he had to come out in the rain.

Ramona sighed. The whole world seemed gray and cross, and it was most unfair that she should have to be dragged along on a dreary ride just because Beezus wanted her hair cut by Dawna. Her mother would never go to all this trouble for Ramona's hair. Huddled in the back seat, she began to feel carsick. The Quimby car, which they had bought from someone who had owned a large dog, began to smell like a dog. "Oh-h," moaned Ramona, feeling sick. She thought about the oatmeal she had eaten for breakfast and quickly tried not to think about it.

Mrs. Quimby glanced in the rear-view mirror. "Are you all right, Ramona?" Her voice was anxious.

Ramona did not answer. She was afraid to open her mouth.

"I think she's going to upchuck," said Beezus, who, since she was in the seventh grade, said *upchuck* instead of *throw up*. She felt the new word was more sophisticated.

"Hang on, Ramona!" said Mrs. Quimby. "I can't stop on the freeway, and there's no way to get off."

"Mother!" cried Beezus. "She's turning green!"

"Ramona, open the window and hang on!" ordered Mrs. Quimby.

Ramona was too miserable to move. Beezus understood. She unbuckled her seat belt, which buzzed angrily. "Oh, shut up," she said to her seat belt as she leaned over and lowered a window for Ramona.

Cold air swept away the doggy smell, and drops of rain against her face made Ramona feel better, but she kept her mouth shut and did not move. Hanging on was not easy.

"How did I ever get into this?" Mrs. Quimby wondered aloud as she turned onto the off-ramp that led from the freeway.

When the haircut expedition finally reached the shopping center and parked near Robert's School of Hair Design, the three Quimbys splashed through the rain. Ramona, who had quickly recovered when the car stopped, found a certain grim pleasure in stomping in puddles with her boots.

After the cold, the air inside the beauty school seemed too warm and too fragrant. Pee-you, thought Ramona as she listened to running water, snipping scissors, and the hushed roar of hair dryers.

A man, probably Robert himself, asked, "What can I do to help you ladies?" as perspiring Ramona began to wiggle out of her car coat.

Beezus was suddenly shy. "I — I would like Dawna to cut my hair," she said in almost a whisper.

"Dawna graduated last week," said Robert, glancing behind the screen that hid the activity of the school, "but Lester can take you."

"Go ahead," said Mrs. Quimby, answering Beezus's questioning eyes. "You want your hair cut."

When Robert asked for payment in advance, Beezus pulled open her crocheted bag and unfolded the bills she had saved. As Robert led her behind the screen, Mrs. Quimby sank with a little sigh into one of the plastic chairs and picked up a shabby magazine. Ramona tried to amuse herself by drawing pictures with her toe in the damp and muddy spots their boots had left on the linoleum.

"Ramona, please don't do that," said Mrs. Quimby, glancing up from her magazine.

Ramona flopped back in a chair and sighed. Her booted feet were beginning to feel hot. To pass the time, she studied pictures of hair styles mounted on the wall. "Is Beezus going to look like *that*?" she whispered.

Mrs. Quimby glanced up again. "I hope not," she whispered back.

Ramona peeked behind the screen and reported to her mother. "A man is washing Beezus's hair, and she's lying back with her head in a sink. He's using gobs of shampoo. He's wasting it."

"Mm-mm." Mrs. Quimby did not raise her eyes from the magazine. Ramona twisted her head to see what her mother found so interesting. Recipes.

Ramona returned for another look. "He's rubbing her hair with a towel," she reported.

"Mm-mm." Ramona disliked her mother's mm-mming. She walked quietly behind the screen to watch. Lester was studying Beezus's hair, one lock at a time, while a woman, probably a teacher, watched.

"Ramona, come back here," Mrs. Quimby whispered from the edge of the screen.

Once more Ramona flopped down in the plastic chair and swung her legs back and forth. How nice it would be if she could have her hair shampooed, too. She raised her eyebrows as high as she could to make her bangs look longer and thought of her quarter, two nickels, and eight pennies at home in a Q-tip box.

"Little girl, would you like to have your hair cut?" asked Robert, as if he had read her mind — or was tired of watching her swing her legs.

Ramona stopped swinging her legs and answered politely, "No, thank you. We are scrimping and pinching to make ends meet." Using "scrimping and pinching" made her feel grown-up.

An exasperated sigh escaped Mrs. Quimby. She glanced at her watch. Beezus's haircut was taking longer than she had planned.

"Haircuts for children under ten are half price," said Robert, "and no waiting. We aren't very busy on a wet morning like this."

Mrs. Quimby studied Ramona's hair while Ramona tried to push her eyebrows still higher. "All right, Ramona," she said. "Your hair does need cutting again, and it will help to have one more Saturday chore out of the way."

In a moment Ramona found herself draped with a poodle-printed plastic sheet and lying back with her hair buried under mounds of lather while a young woman named Denise rubbed her scalp. Such bliss! Washing hair at home was never like this. No soap in her eyes, no having to complain that the water was too hot or too cold, no bumping her head on the kitchen faucet while her knees ached from kneeling on a chair, no one telling her to stop wiggling, no water dribbling down her neck. The shampoo was over much too soon. Denise rubbed Ramona's hair with a towel and guided her to a chair in front of a mirror. On the other side of the row of mirrors, she could hear Beezus's hair being snipped with long pauses between snips.

"She's definitely the pixie type," said the teacher to Denise.

Me? thought Ramona, surprised and pleased. Ramona the pixie sounded much nicer than Ramona the pest as she had so often been called by Beezus and her friends.

"A little off the bangs," said the teacher, "and the ends tapered."

Denise went to work. Her scissors flashed and snipped. Unlike Lester on the other side of the mirror, Denise was sure of what she was doing. Perhaps she had studied longer.

Ramona closed her eyes. *Snip-snip-snip* went her bangs. When she opened her eyes she was surprised to discover they were a tiny bit longer in the center of her forehead. Like the top of a heart, thought Ramona, like a valentine.

Denise lifted locks of wet hair between her fingers and snipped with flying scissors. Lift and snip, all the way around Ramona's head. Flicks of a comb, and

Denise aimed a hand-held hair dryer at Ramona's head with one hand while she guided Ramona's hair into place with a brush held in the other. In no time Ramona's hair was dry. More flicks of the comb, the plastic sheet was whisked away, and there sat Ramona with shining hair neatly shaped to her head.

"Excellent," said the teacher to Denise. "She looks adorable."

Students who had no customers gathered around. Ramona could not believe the words she was hearing. "Darling." "Cute as a bug." "A real little pixie." The dryer was humming on the other side of the mirror.

Ramona felt light and happy when she returned to her mother.

"Why, Ramona!" said Mrs. Quimby, laying aside her magazine. "Your hair looks lovely. So neat and shiny."

Ramona couldn't stop smiling, she was so happy. She twitched her nose with joy.

But something made the smile on Mrs. Quimby's face fade. Ramona turned and stared at Beezus standing beside the screen. Her sister's hair had been teased and sprayed until it stood up three inches above her face. Her bangs were plastered in a curve across her forehead. Beezus did not look like an ice skater on television. She looked like an unhappy seventh-grade girl with forty-year-old hair.

Ramona did not know what to say. No one knew what to say except Robert. "You look lovely, dear," he said, but no one answered. Beezus's face looked stiff as her hair.

Ramona thought of the allowance Beezus had saved and wanted to shout at Robert, "She does not look lovely! My sister looks terrible!" For once she kept still. She felt sorry for her sister and sad about the allowance she had saved for so long, but deep inside, where she was ashamed of her feeling, she felt a tiny triumph. Ramona looked nicer than Beezus.

Ramona walked carefully to the car, not wanting to disturb her hair by running and hopping. Beezus walked in stony silence. When all three had buckled their seat belts, Beezus could no longer hold back her feelings. "Well, go ahead and say it!" she burst out in anger and in tears. "Tell me my hair looks terrible. Tell me my hair looks stiff and horrible, like a wig. A *cheap* wig!"

"Now Beezus." Mrs. Quimby spoke gently.

"Well, it *does!* You know it does," Beezus went on. "I tried to tell the man I didn't want my hair to stand up, but he said I would be pleased when he finished, and now I've wasted your whole morning and all my allowance. I look terrible and can't go to school because everyone will laugh at me." She began to sob.

"Dear girl —" Mrs. Quimby took Beezus in her arms and let her weep against her shoulder.

Tears came into Ramona's eyes. She felt she could not bear her sister's unhappiness even if she did look nicer than Beezus. That awful stiff hair, the wasted allowance. . . . Ramona no longer triumphed in looking nicer. She did not want to look nicer. She wanted them to look the same so people would say, There goes that nice-looking Beatrice Quimby and her nice-looking little sister.

"I j-just wanted to look nice." Beezus's voice was muffled by her mother's coat. "I know th-that what I do is more important than how I look, but I just wanted to look nice."

"Of course you do," soothed Mrs. Quimby. "No matter what we say, we all want to look nice."

Ramona sniffed, she felt so sad.

"And you will look nice," Mrs. Quimby continued, "once you wash out all that hair spray and comb your hair. Don't forget Lester cut your hair, and that's what counts."

Beezus raised her soggy tear-stained face. "Do you really think it will look all right when it's washed?"

"Yes, I do," said Mrs. Quimby. "It just needs to be washed and combed."

Beezus sat up and let out an exhausted sigh. Mother and daughter had forgotten their adorable pixie buckled down in the corner of the back seat. Ramona hoped she could make it home without upchucking. She did not want to muss her hair.

Beverly Cleary, age 7

About the Author
Beverly Cleary

Beverly Cleary has written more books about Ramona Quimby than about any other character. Perhaps it's because she and Ramona have so much in common. As a child, Cleary had straight brown hair, which she always wore short. She loved to read and go to the library. And, like Ramona, Cleary even used to get motion sickness whenever she rode in a car.

Alan Tiegreen, age 9

About the Illustrator
Alan Tiegreen

There's a scene in *Ramona Quimby, Age 8* where Ramona and Beezus make a mess out of the kitchen. It's Alan Tiegreen's favorite illustration because it reminds him of the time years ago when he spilled water in the big sugar bin in the kitchen. He tried adding more water to smooth out the sugar, but he ended up making an even bigger mess.

254

Choose Your Own Style

Share an Experience

Hair-Raising Stories

What's the worst haircut you've ever received? Did you feel like Beezus afterward? Tell your bad haircut story to a small group. You might want to draw a picture of how you looked.

Make an Advertisement

Wash, Cut, and Dry

Create an advertisement for Robert's School of Hair Design. Make a poster, design a billboard, or choose another kind of ad. Include a picture of Ramona or a quote of what she might say about her haircut.

My Own Room
A Persuasive Essay by Andy Costa

Have you ever wanted a room of your own? Andy did. Here's how he tried to persuade his parents.

My Own Room

I should have my own bedroom because I need privacy, I would get more sleep, and I need more space for my things. Michael and I have shared a room for nine-and-a-half years, but it's time to split. It was fun to have somebody to talk to before I fell asleep, but now I'm older and more mature.

I need privacy when I have friends over and when I'm doing my homework. Michael's stereo is so loud that I can't talk to friends or concentrate on my work. If I had my own room, I could close my door whenever I felt like it!

I need my own room because Michael has to get up earlier than I do. His alarm wakes me up when I could be asleep. If I had my own bedroom, I would get an extra two-and-a-half hours sleep each week.

I need space for my clothes, toys, and junk. Michael takes up more than his share of the room. His school supplies and sports equipment take up too much space. If I had my own room, I would have my own closet and shelves all to myself.

I could move into the room that is now the guest room. Perhaps you could take out certain things so that I would have room for all of my games and books. When Grandmother and Granddaddy visit, I would let them sleep in my new room.

I think you should give me my own bedroom for all of these reasons.

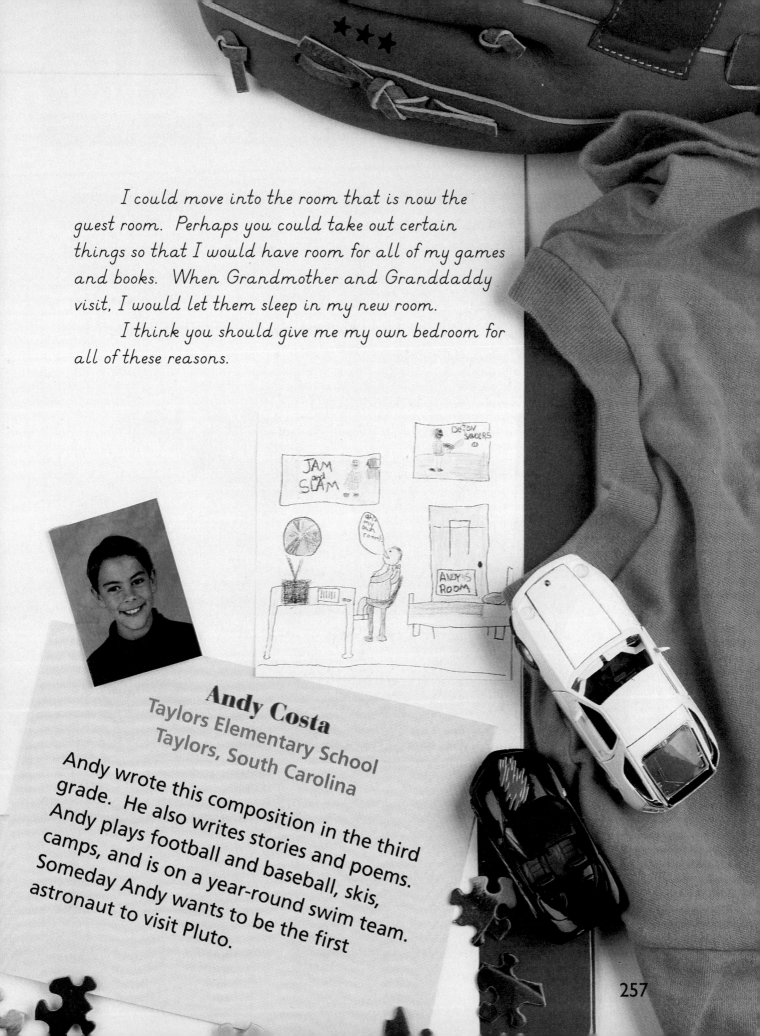

Andy Costa
Taylors Elementary School
Taylors, South Carolina

Andy wrote this composition in the third grade. He also writes stories and poems. Andy plays football and baseball, skis, camps, and is on a year-round swim team. Someday Andy wants to be the first astronaut to visit Pluto.

A Calendar for Kids

by Margo McLoone-Basta and Alice Siegel

The days of the year would be pretty dull if they were simply numbered from 1 to 365 without special holidays, birthdays, and events. This calendar was designed just for kids to celebrate the serious as well as the silly days of the year. Make each day special by discovering a new fact, remembering an important person, or amusing yourself with an off-beat celebration.

January

3 Sip-Through-a-Straw-Day

The drinking straw was patented on this day in 1888.

20 Hat Day

This is the day to celebrate the many kinds of hats worn by the people of the world.

30 Swap-the-Brown-Bag-Lunch-Day

To liven up lunchtime, exchange lunch with a friend.

February

11 National Inventors Day

14 Valentine's Day

March

1 National Pig Day

22 National Goof-Off Day

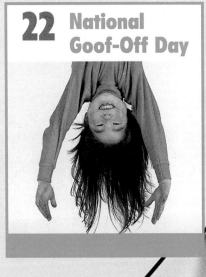

April

11

On this day in 1947, Jackie Robinson joined the Brooklyn Dodgers as the first black major league baseball player.

22 Earth Day

259

May

1 May Day

A day for May baskets, maypoles, and flower festivals.

5 Cinco de Mayo

This Mexican national holiday celebrates the Mexican victory over the French in the Battle of Puebla, 1867.

2

The first night baseball game was played in Fort Wayne, Indiana, in 1883.

18 International Picnic Day

30

On this day in 1859, a French acrobat and aerialist, Charles Blondin, walked across Niagra Falls on a tightrope.

July

4 Happy Birthday U.S.A.

The United States of America was born in 1776.

15 National Ice Cream Day

20

The first people to land on the moon were Americans Neil Armstrong and Edwin "Buzz" Aldrin, Jr., in 1969.

August

5 Family Day

13 International Left-Handers Day

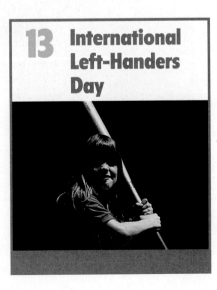

261

September

5 National Be Late for Something Day

12 Snack-a-Pickle Day

19

In 1928, Mickey Mouse appeared in his first movie, *Steamboat Willie.*

October

20

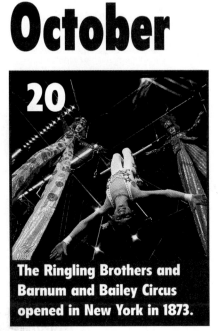

The Ringling Brothers and Barnum and Bailey Circus opened in New York in 1873.

28

The Statue of Liberty was dedicated on this day in 1886.

November

17 Homemade Bread Day

Enjoy the making and eating of homemade bread.

21 World Hello Day

Hola

Hello

Jambo

Konnichiwa

Bonjour

Shalom

December

17

In 1903, Americans Orville and Wilbur Wright made the first successful airplane flight.

22 International Arbor Day

This is the day to promote the planting and preserving of trees around the world.

28

American William Semple patented chewing gum on this day in 1869.

263

About the Author
Elizabeth Fitzgerald Howard

All of the books Elizabeth Fitzgerald Howard writes are based on true stories. *Mac & Marie & the Train Toss Surprise* is about one of the many adventures her father had growing up in a big house near a railroad track in Patapsco, Maryland.

About the Illustrator
Gail Gordon Carter

Gail Gordon Carter grew up in Los Angeles, California, the oldest of three girls. Today she lives in Portland, Oregon, with her husband and young daughter. Her illustrations for this book were done with watercolors and colored pencils.

MAC & MARIE & the TRAIN TOSS SURPRISE

by ELIZABETH FITZGERALD HOWARD

illustrations by GAIL GORDON CARTER

It was beginning to get dark. Mac was sure that Marie was tired of waiting. He had watched her catch six fireflies and put them in a jelly jar, clamping the lid on tight each time. Mac had punched holes in the lid. Marie had put some grass in, too; she said it was in case the fireflies were hungry. Mac knew that Marie knew that fireflies didn't really eat grass. Marie was just playing around, trying to pass the time.

Tiger, Mac's old collie, was watching Marie, too. Tiger didn't run after fireflies. He might chase a rabbit if he smelled one. Or he might just lie there, with his ears back, lazy and comfortable. Waiting.

"It'll be soon now, Marie." Mac checked Papa's big pocket watch. "About five more minutes, if it's on time." Mac sat up straight. He had been sprawled out in the tall grass near the railroad embankment, chewing on a cat-o'-nine-tails stem. Mac wasn't as fidgety as Marie. He was older, and besides, he knew most of the train schedules by heart. Mac knew about trains.

Marie stopped chasing fireflies. She stared down the long tracks. Then she turned impatiently, twisted the lid off the fireflies jar, and dumped them out. She watched them fly away, flickering their lights.

"Hey, Mac! What if it's all a big trick?"

"But you saw Uncle Clem's letter," Mac answered.

"Maybe he's fooling us — making us all excited about some silly old surprise."

"Oh, come on, Marie. Why would he tell us exactly the name of the train and the time and everything?" What does Marie know anyway? Mac thought.

Mac pulled the scrunched-up piece of paper from his back pocket. Uncle Clem's letter. Almost too dark to read, but Mac could remember every word.

Dear Mac,

*I have a summer job in the dining car on the Seaboard
Florida Limited. We'll be passing by the Big House,
heading back to New York, a bit after half-past eight
on Thursday night. I'm going to throw something off
for you. It's for Marie, too. Wrapped in white paper
and tied with string. Just be sure you pick it up!*

*Love,
Uncle Clem*

Uncle Clem was Mac's favorite relative. Uncle Clem went to college in New York. And now, even better, he had a summer job on a train.

More than anything, Mac loved trains. He wanted to ride on them, to see where those long, silvery tracks went. And when he grew up, he would get a job on the trains, too.

Marie was right, though. Sometimes Uncle Clem did play jokes, like the time no one was expecting him, and he hid in the hall closet all through dinner and then jumped out during dessert and almost scared Mama and Marie out of their wits! Mac had thought that was a pretty funny trick.

But this wouldn't be a trick. Not tonight.

"What's it going to be, Uncle Clem's surprise?" Marie asked. "If he's working in the dining car, what's it going to be?"

"Maybe some steak they don't need," Mac said. But he didn't really think so.

"Hey, Mac, what about a big chocolate cake? Or maybe a pie?"

"Better be squash pie," Mac teased. "It'll sure squash when it lands in the bushes."

Marie laughed.

Mac stared down the tracks as far as he could. He had lived close to the train tracks almost since he could remember, and now he was nine. Papa had bought the Big House — everyone called it that — when Mac was still practically a baby. It was a nice house. Once Mama got a letter from the railroad people saying the Big House was the prettiest place on the line between Baltimore and Washington.

273

Mac liked the house, especially the two big porches. The one in front was called the Flower Porch. You could sit there and admire Mama's flower garden. Now the garden was full of daylilies and hollyhocks. The second porch, the best porch, on the back, Mac had named the Train Porch. It faced the railroad tracks. There you could wait for the trains to come. Watch them zoom by. Mac liked it at night, too. Lying upstairs in bed he'd listen for the far-off whistle and then the *clack-a-clacky* sounds of the night trains speeding past.

There were a few local trains just between Baltimore and Washington. They were shorter and slower and stopped at little towns like Laurel and Halethorpe and Patapsco, near the Big House. But the long trains, the really fast trains, went north to Boston, even to Bar Harbor, Maine. And on the other track,

they went south, through Washington, D.C., and Virginia, and both Carolinas, and Georgia, ending up in Florida. Mac knew the names of all the long trains. The *Merchants Limited*. The *Royal Blue Flyer*. The *Federal*. The *Colonial*. The *Florida Fast Mail*. The *Keystone Express*. The *New York Special*. And Uncle Clem's train, the *Seaboard Florida Limited*.

Someday, someday . . . Mac would be working on those trains. Going everywhere. Seeing the world. Way up north to Bar Harbor, Maine. Way down south. To Florida. Maybe out west, even. California! And not working in the dining car, like Uncle Clem, even though Uncle Clem was the luckiest person in the world. I'm going to be a fireman, and then I'm going to be an engineer, Mac thought.

"Hey, Mac! Mac! What time is it?" Marie asked.

Mac squinted at Papa's watch. "Twenty-five minutes to nine."
Three more minutes now. But would Uncle Clem really throw
something off? Mac worried a little bit. If it was food, would that
be right? Would it be leftovers? Maybe from people's plates? No,
Uncle Clem wouldn't do that. Unless it was a bone for Tiger. But
Uncle Clem had said it was something for him and Marie.

"It's so quiet," Marie said. "I can hear a worm walking. I can
hear ants dancing. I can hear moles moving in their holes."

"Just nighttime noises," Mac said softly.

A whippoorwill called out. An owl hooted. *Swoosh!*

"What was that? A bat?" Marie moved closer to Mac.

"Listen! Listen!" Mac said suddenly. "Can you hear it now?"
A train whistle whined way down the tracks.

"All right! That's it!" Mac shouted.

"That's it!" Marie echoed. "Be careful, Mac!"

The round light on the front of the engine grew larger
and larger and brighter and brighter. The whistle grew louder.
There was smoke and whirling sparks and the hissing of steam.
"Yippee!" Mac yelled. He counted the cars flashing by. "Dining
car!" he shouted into the darkness. Was that a silhouette, a shadow
of someone standing at the end of the dining car? "Uncle Clem!"
Mac screamed, waving his arms. And yes, there was something
tossed off, something flying into the sky . . . something flying up
and down again. "Uncle Clem! Uncle Clem!" Mac called, and
the train was gone.

"I saw it!" shouted Marie. "I saw a package in the air!"

"Over this way," Mac said, scrambling down the embankment, snatching hold of slippery weeds. "You wait there, Marie. I can get it." Mac had to be careful near the tracks. At least he knew that the next train wouldn't be due for a whole hour.

Where was that package? Tiger was barking and sniffing. *Where was it?*

"Marie, I see it! I see the package!" And there, partly hidden in the weeds, was the lumpy, white bundle. Smaller than a bed pillow. Bigger than a loaf pan. Tied with brown string. Mack picked it up. He and Tiger clambered back up to Marie.

"Is it a big chocolate cake, Mac? Let me smell it!" Marie tried to pull the package out of Mac's hands.

"Doesn't feel like food, Marie. Let's take it back to the Big House to open it."

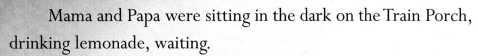

Mama and Papa were sitting in the dark on the Train Porch, drinking lemonade, waiting.

"Well, well, so Clem tossed something off for you. . . Well, let's see it," said Papa. Mama went into the house for the oil lamp.

Mac dug and pulled at the string until he got all the knots out. Marie helped him unwrap the layers and layers of white paper. "Clem sure didn't want whatever it is to break. I've never seen so much wrapping," said Mama.

At last.

It was mottled, pinkish and brown, bumpy-rough on the outside, and smooth, shiny pink on the inside. Wider at the open end. And it curved around.

"It's a seashell!" Marie and Mac shouted in one shout. "A *giant* seashell!" Mac added. "And here's a letter, too." Tucked in the shell was a piece of folded paper. Mac read:

Dear Mac and Marie,

This is a conch shell from Florida.

Maybe you can hear the ocean.

Bye,
Uncle Clem

P. S. Watch for the train next Thursday night!

Mac smoothed his hands all over the big shell, tracing the bumps and curves with his fingers. Marie held it, too, turning it around, carefully, carefully. "Pink," she said. "Inside it's pink." Then Mac held the shell up to his ear. "I can hear it! The ocean!" he said. Marie listened, too. And so did Mama and Papa.

"Uncle Clem got you a little piece of Florida," Papa said. "Now that's a real nice surprise."

Mac listened some more to the ocean sound. He smiled at the beautiful shell. He smiled at Mama and Papa and Marie. "When I'm an engineer on the train to Florida," he said, "I'm going to bring back surprises from the world, too — just like Uncle Clem."

A boyhood photo of the author's father, John MacFarland ("Mac") Fitzgerald, on whom this story is based

Mac swinging with the children of family friends during a summer get-together at the Big House

286

More Surprises

Role-Play a Scene

Uncle Clem Returns

With a group, act out a scene of Uncle Clem's next visit with Mac's family. What new places has Uncle Clem traveled to? How might Mac and Marie express their appreciation for his gift?

Find a Gift

Where's That From?

If Uncle Clem visited *your* part of the country, what gift would he bring back? Find a gift from your area, such as a unique rock, flower, or leaf. Surprise someone with the gift and a note explaining where you found it.

Out Island Sean

Amos Ferguson

That Kind of Day

It's that kind of day
and that kind of season
when the breeze is sweet
and the cool air calls
"Come out!"
It beckons the folks
who come out of doors
and wander about
pretending at first
to look for chores
although they know
they just want to walk
in the breeze and the pale
sunlight
it's that kind of day

Eloise Greenfield

What a Day I Had!

Four Kids Tell Their Incredible Stories.

Wash Day

Jamie Coleman
North Jackson Elementary
Jackson, Mississippi

One day last summer my washing machine went crazy.

I was washing my parents' clothes. After I started the clothes, I went to get some cookies and milk. I heard a loud knocking noise, so I ran back to the laundry room. The washing machine was bouncing up and down.

I ran to my mom's room and told her to come quickly. We hurried back and saw the washing machine squirting water everywhere. When we tried to turn the machine off, we got soaking wet. Finally, my mom turned it off.

Water had sprayed all over the floor and the walls. I mopped the water and my mom called my dad at work. My dad came home and fixed the washing machine.

Then I finished washing clothes. Finally, I ate my cookies and milk!

Coming to America

Matthew Uckotter
Clays Mill Elementary
Lexington, Kentucky

One day, when I lived in Korea, my mom could not afford to keep me. So, she took me to the orphanage and dropped me off there. A while later a man from the orphanage took me to the airport. I felt scared because I didn't understand where I was going and I couldn't speak his language.

It was my first time to be on an airplane, and I thought it was neat. But the trip lasted a long time, almost twelve hours, and I got airsick. I was glad to finally get off that plane! I walked into the airport and looked around. Standing in the lobby was my new family, the Uckotters.

My new mom hugged me, and Dad carried me to the car. Everything seemed so weird and scary! Then we drove to my new house in Lexington, Kentucky. In my mind I said, "Wow, this is so different than my other house."

We had a party to celebrate my arrival, and Mom served cake and cola. After I drank the cup of cola, I was jumping for more! I ran around the room, shouting, "Cola, cola!" That was my first English word. Everyone thought I was cute and funny, and I knew I would be happy in my new home.

291

My Worst Day

Beverly Hernandez
Mountainside Elementary
Fort Carson, Colorado

My worst day was when it was Christmas Day.

My brother was the first one up from bed. He went downstairs to look at our fish tank. First he saw the presents under the tree. He opened all the presents that were marked for him.

Then he went to look at the fish tank. He screamed when he saw that one of my fish was eating a bug!

My parents and I ran downstairs. As soon as we were down there, my brother said, "I'm going to kill that bug." He dropped a piece of wrapping paper into the tank.

"No!" I yelled. It was too late. The glue-covered wrapping paper was already getting soft.

The next day, all the fish had died. And that was because of my little brother!

Going Bowling

Joe Sturdivant
Clays Mill Elementary
Lexington, Kentucky

When I was at Bryan's house one Saturday, his dad said, "Let's go bowling!"

At the bowling alley we picked out our shoes, got our bowling ball, and found our lane. When it was my turn to bowl, I got ready, and pulled the ball behind me . . . BOOM! When I brought my arm forward, the ball wasn't there!

Everyone turned and stared at me, and I was really embarrassed. I turned around and saw my ball way back where the seats were. I had to go get it and start over.

This time, I rolled the ball slowly, and I bowled a strike. An old lady, who was a great bowler, gave me a high five, and I felt proud. When it was my turn again, I bowled a spare, which made my score 44.

Then, on my next try, I only hit one pin. Just when I thought I was a terrible bowler, I bowled a strike again.

Bryan's dad said, "Joe, you're a good bowler." Even though I was embarrassed when I dropped the ball, I had to agree with him — I am a good bowler!

293

Meet GAIL GIBBONS

Gail Gibbons has this advice for young writers: "Write about something you know about. Write about what you like. You'll enjoy it a lot more!"

Gibbons follows her own advice. She loves going to the movies, so she wrote *Lights! Camera! Action! How a Movie Is Made*. Because she lives part of the year on an island in Maine, she wrote *Surrounded by Sea: Life on a New England Fishing Island*. And her love for animals has led her to write many books about them, including *Say Woof! The Day of a Country Veterinarian*.

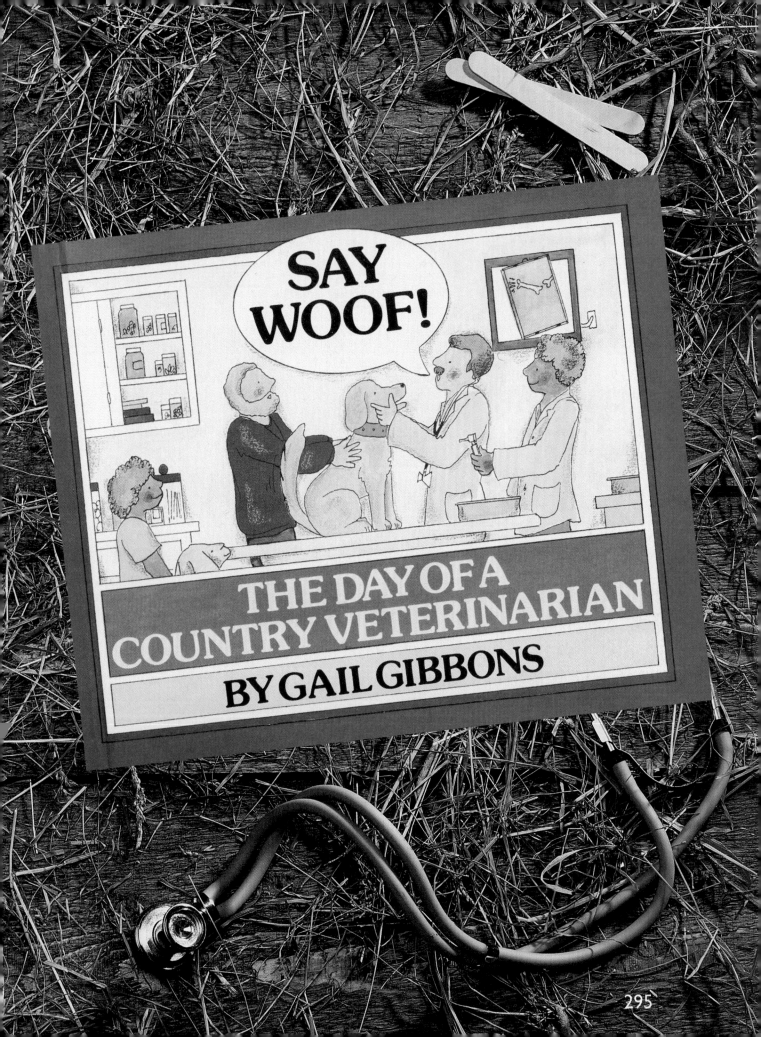

A dog, a kitten, a baby goat, a parakeet and another
dog. They are all patients at the animal hospital. It is
early morning, but people and their pets are already here.

They are waiting to see the veterinarian. A
veterinarian is a doctor who takes care of animals, the
way other doctors take care of people.

This country veterinarian loves animals and wants to help them. Before he could open his own animal hospital, he had to go to a special school after college, just as a doctor goes to medical school. He had to learn how to care for many different kinds of animals — pets and farm animals.

Before he sees his patients, the vet checks the animals that have stayed overnight. Some of them are boarders, staying at the animal hospital while their owners are away from home. Others are there because they are patients. The vet checks on a dog he operated on yesterday. All is well. Soon her owner will come to get her. An assistant has just finished cleaning their cages. She gives them fresh water and feeds the ones that need to be fed.

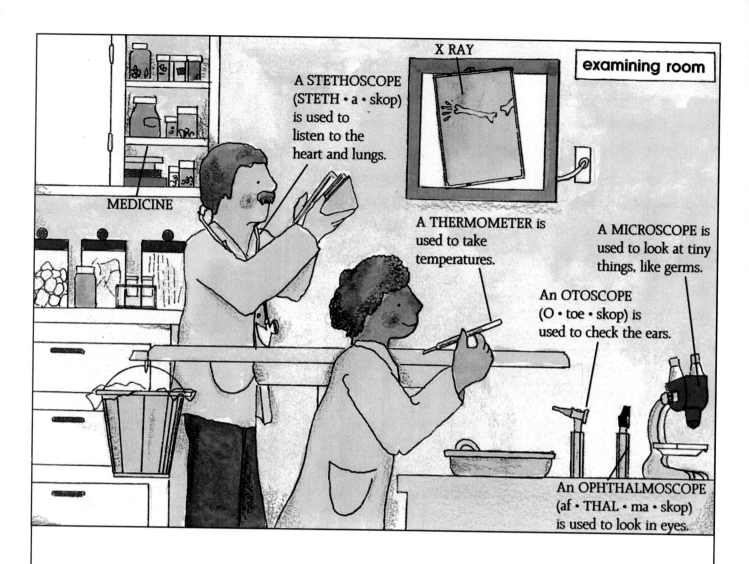

A STETHOSCOPE (STETH · a · skop) is used to listen to the heart and lungs.

X RAY

examining room

MEDICINE

A THERMOMETER is used to take temperatures.

A MICROSCOPE is used to look at tiny things, like germs.

An OTOSCOPE (O · toe · skop) is used to check the ears.

An OPHTHALMOSCOPE (af · THAL · ma · skop) is used to look in eyes.

It's nine o'clock. Office hours have begun. The vet checks the appointment book in his examining room. His other assistant makes sure all the medical tools are clean and ready.

The SPLINT straightens and braces the wing.

Here's the first patient, a parakeet with a broken wing. The owner tells the vet that her bird flew into a wall. The vet gently feels where the break is and carefully puts a splint on it. "Come back in five days," he tells her. "I'll see how the wing is mending."

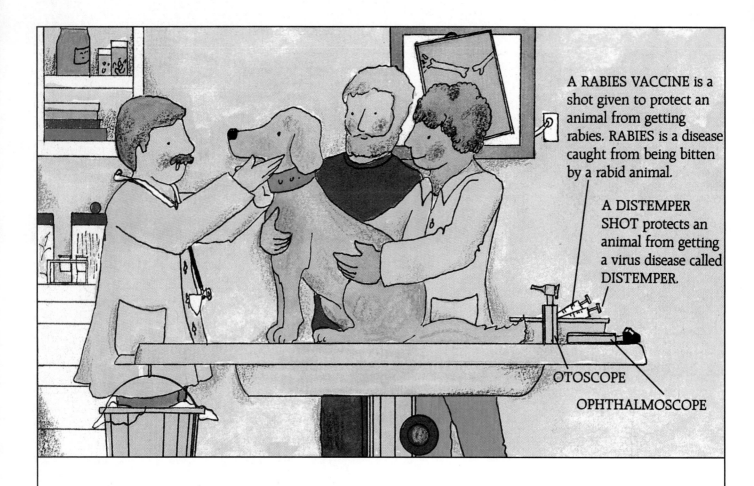

A RABIES VACCINE is a shot given to protect an animal from getting rabies. RABIES is a disease caught from being bitten by a rabid animal.

A DISTEMPER SHOT protects an animal from getting a virus disease called DISTEMPER.

OTOSCOPE

OPHTHALMOSCOPE

"Wilton is next," the assistant calls. Wilton is here for his yearly checkup. The vet examines his eyes and ears. He looks at the dog's fur. "Say woof!" the vet jokes as he looks down Wilton's throat. Next, the vet touches and feels his body and takes his temperature. Wilton is a healthy dog. All he needs to get is a rabies vaccine and distemper shot.

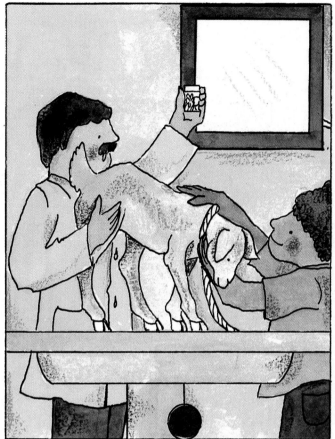

Who's next? A cute kitten! The vet examines him. He is in good health and only needs the few shots that all kittens are supposed to have. The next patient is a baby goat. She has a stomachache and won't eat. The vet looks her over and tells the owner she will be fine. "Just give her these pills three times a day," he says.

SET means to put back in its correct position.

Emergency! Someone has just brought in a baby groundhog that was hit by a truck. It has a broken leg. The vet sets and splints the leg and tells his assistant to put the animal in one of the cages. Finally, he examines the dog that has been so patient out in the waiting room. She has an eye infection. "Put this ointment on her eye each day for a week. Then come back to see me," he tells the owner.

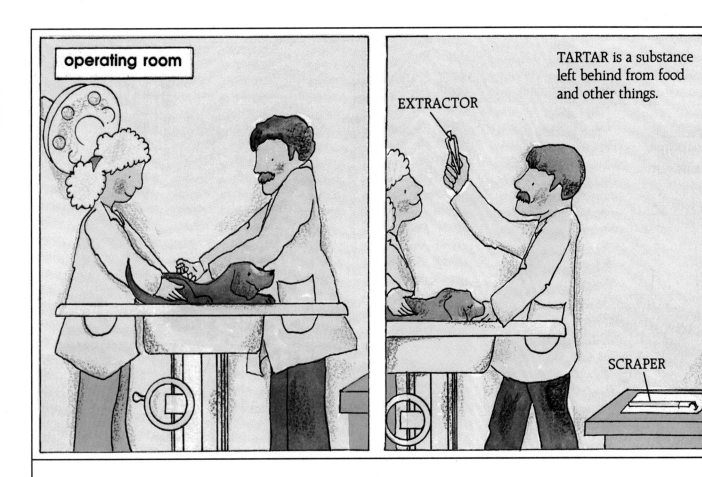

It's eleven o'clock. Surgery time. Two pets were boarded overnight because they are scheduled for surgery today. The first patient's name is Ben. Poor Ben has a toothache. The vet gives him a shot to put him to sleep. Then he finds Ben's bad tooth and pulls it out. While Ben is still asleep, the vet cleans the tartar from the rest of his teeth so they won't become infected.

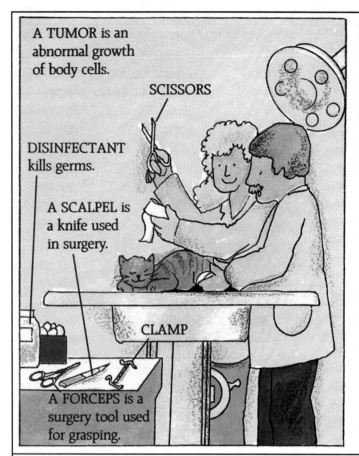

A TUMOR is an abnormal growth of body cells.

SCISSORS

DISINFECTANT kills germs.

A SCALPEL is a knife used in surgery.

CLAMP

A FORCEPS is a surgery tool used for grasping.

The other patient is a cat. She has a lump called a tumor on her leg. After her shot, she falls asleep. Slowly the vet cuts the tumor away and removes it. Then the cut is sutured, or stitched. The area is disinfected and bandaged with soft tape. They place her carefully back in her cage.

What a busy morning! Time to relax and have some lunch. The phone rings. It's another vet in a nearby town. She wants to know about a new medicine the vet has been using. Veterinarians must stay up to date on the latest medical improvements.

Country vets only spend part of their days in their offices. The rest of the time they are on the road taking care of animals on farms, at stables, and in homes. The vet checks his schedule book. Then he gathers up the blood samples he's taken from some of his patients to bring to a medical lab.

Outside, one of his assistants is at the truck, filling it
with everything the vet might need to treat the animals
they will see. Off they go.

BLOOD
SAMPLE

BRUCELLOSIS (brew · sa · LOW · sis)
is a disease that causes fever
in cattle and people.

It's one-thirty. First stop. They arrive at a farm
where the vet takes blood samples from the farmer's
cows. This blood will be tested at a state lab to see if the
cows have a disease called brucellosis. A farmer cannot
sell milk or sell his cows for meat if they have this
disease.

The next stop is a stable. One of the horses has a
sore, lame leg. The vet gives her a shot to kill the pain.
"I'll stop by tomorrow to see how she is doing," the
vet says.

ANEMIC means there aren't enough red blood cells.

At the next stop a farmer has some new baby pigs. "Could you look them over?" the farmer asks. They squeal as the vet and his assistant check them. Each one gets an iron shot so they won't become anemic. They are very healthy piglets.

The next farm is a sheep farm. The vet cuts off, or docks, the lambs' tails. If he doesn't, their tails would get dirty and attract lots of flies that would bother them. It's best to do this when they are lambs because it doesn't hurt as much as it would when fully grown. The vet and the assistant hug each lamb. "Everything will be okay," they say.

A voice comes from the vet's truck. "Emergency!"
Back at the office the assistant is calling the vet over a
special radio. "Yes?" he answers.

"Mrs. Miller's dog was just hit by a car. Please hurry
over there!" the assistant says.

The vet and his assistant jump into the truck. Off
they go!

Mrs. Miller is very upset. The vet gently feels her
dog's body and legs to see if there are any broken bones.
He listens with his stethoscope. All is well.

The vet looks into the dog's eyes. Then, he notes the color of its gums. They are nice and pink.

"He's more stunned than anything," the vet tells Mrs. Miller. "He should be fine by tomorrow."

It's four-thirty. They stop at the lab to drop off
the blood samples. The lab will have a report ready
tomorrow. Then they head back to the office.

What a long day. It's six o'clock. The vet visits his
two surgery patients in their cages. They're doing well
and will be able to go home to their families tomorrow.
He looks over his day book, the book he wrote in
when he visited places today. He checks tomorrow's
schedule, too.

One of the assistants jots down bills that have been paid. Cages are cleaned and the animals get fresh water. The little groundhog is doing fine. When he is older and all better, the vet plans to release him back into his natural home, the fields in the countryside.

It's time for the country veterinarian and his assistants to go home. Tonight might bring another emergency. If not, tomorrow will be another busy day of caring for animals.

All in a Day's Work

Create a Schedule

Another Busy Day

Use the events, picture clues, and times from the selection to help you write a schedule of a veterinarian's day. Include an activity for each hour or half hour.

Make a Picture Dictionary

Tools of the Trade

Work with a team to make a picture dictionary of the equipment a veterinarian uses. Draw pictures of the instruments, and label each one with its name and purpose.

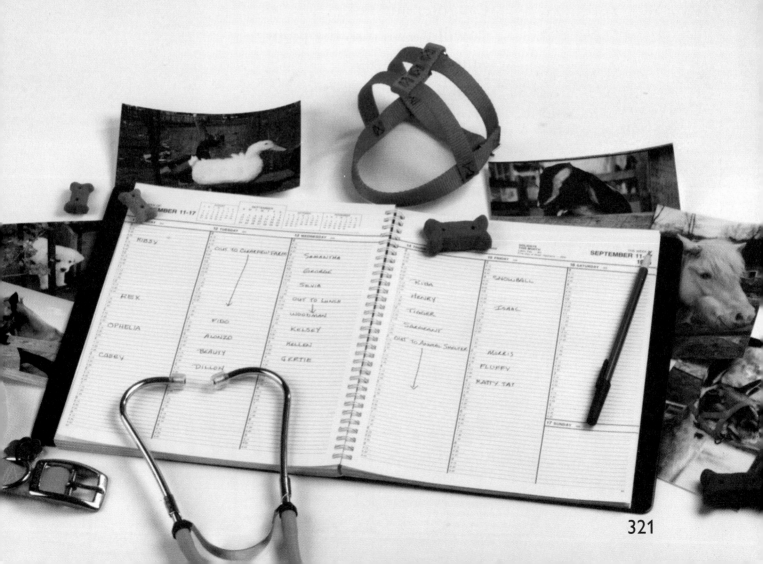

Celebration

I shall dance tonight.
When the dusk comes crawling,
There will be dancing
    and feasting.
I shall dance with the others
    in circles,
        in leaps,
            in stomps.
Laughter and talk
    will weave into the night,
Among the fires
    of my people.
Games will be played
And I shall be
    a part of it.

Alonzo Lopez
illustration by Tomie dePaola

PEANUTS

BY CHARLES M. SCHULZ

Some of the words in this book may have pronunciations or meanings you do not know. This glossary can help you by telling you how to pronounce those words and by telling you the meanings for the words as they are used in this book.

You can find out how to pronounce any glossary word by using the special spelling after the word and the key that runs across the bottom of the glossary pages.

The full pronunciation key on the next page shows how to pronounce each consonant and vowel in a special spelling. The pronunciation key at the bottom of the glossary pages is a shortened form of the full key.

Full Pronunciation Key

Consonant Sounds

b	**b**i**b**, ca**bb**age	kw	**ch**oir, **qu**ick	t	**t**igh**t**, stopp**ed**
ch	**ch**ur**ch**, sti**tch**	l	**l**id, need**le**, ta**ll**	th	ba**th**, **th**in
d	**d**ee**d**, maile**d**, pu**dd**le	m	a**m**, **m**an, du**mb**	*th*	ba**the**, **th**is
f	**f**ast, **f**i**fe**, o**ff**, **ph**rase, rou**gh**	n	**n**o, sudd**en**	v	ca**ve**, val**ve**, **v**ine
		ng	thi**ng**, i**nk**	w	**w**ith, **w**olf
g	**g**a**g**, **g**et, fin**g**er	p	**p**o**p**, ha**pp**y	y	**y**es, **y**olk, on**i**on
h	**h**at, **wh**o	r	**r**oar, **rh**yme	z	ro**s**e, si**z**e, **x**ylophone, **z**ebra
hw	**wh**ich, **wh**ere	s	mi**ss**, **s**au**c**e, **sc**ene, **s**ee	zh	gara**g**e, plea**s**ure, vi**s**ion
j	**j**u**dg**e, **g**em	sh	di**sh**, **sh**ip, **s**ugar, ti**ss**ue		
k	**c**at, **k**i**ck**, s**ch**ool				

Vowel Sounds

ă	r**a**t, l**au**gh	ŏ	h**o**rrible, p**o**t	ŭ	c**u**t, fl**oo**d, r**ou**gh, s**o**me
ā	**a**pe, **ai**d, p**ay**	ō	g**o**, r**ow**, t**oe**, th**ough**		
â	**ai**r, c**a**re, w**ea**r			û	c**i**rcle, f**u**r, h**ea**rd, t**e**rm, t**u**rn, **u**rge, w**o**rd
ä	f**a**ther, k**o**ala, y**a**rd	ô	**a**ll, c**au**ght, f**o**r, p**aw**		
ĕ	p**e**t, pl**ea**sure, **a**ny	oi	b**oy**, n**oi**se, **oi**l	y$\overline{oo}$	c**u**re
ē	b**e**, b**ee**, **ea**sy, p**ia**no	ou	c**ow**, **ou**t	y$\overline{oo}$	ab**u**se, **u**se
ĭ	**i**f, p**i**t, b**u**sy	$\overline{oo}$	f**u**ll, t**oo**k, w**o**lf	ə	**a**bout, sil**e**nt, penc**i**l, lem**o**n, circ**u**s
ī	b**y**, p**ie**, h**igh**	$\overline{oo}$	b**oo**t, fr**ui**t, fl**ew**		
î	d**ea**r, d**ee**r, f**ie**rce, m**e**re				

Stress marks

Primary Stress ′: bi•ol•o•gy [bī **ŏl**′ ə jē]

Secondary Stress ′: bi•o•log•i•cal [bī′ ə **lŏj**′ i kəl]

Pronunciation key © 1993 by Houghton Mifflin Company. Adapted and reprinted by permission from *The American Heritage Children's Dictionary.*

A

C

ad•o•ra•tion (ăd´ ə rā´ shən) *noun*
Great love: *The bride and groom gave each other rings to show their **adoration** for each other.*

a•lert (ə **lûrt**´) *noun* A warning: *The siren on an ambulance is an **alert** to people driving cars or crossing the street.*

ALERT

Alert comes from the Italian *all'erta*, meaning "on the watch."

---

a•pol•o•gize (ə **pŏl**´ ə jīz´) *verb*
To say that one is sorry: *Nicole **apologized** to Malcolm for having lost his library book.*

ar•gu•ment (är´ gyə mənt) *noun*
A disagreement: *The two boys had an **argument** about what to watch on TV.*

as•sure (ə **shŏŏr**´) *verb* To make certain: *The teacher **assured** me that if I studied, I would do well on the test.*

car (kär) *noun* **1.** An automobile: *Mom drives her **car** to work, but Dad takes a train.* **2.** A section of a train: *A freight train has many **cars** for carrying goods.*

freight cars

CAR

In ancient times, the Celts (who lived in Europe) had a kind of wagon called a *karros*. It was used to move armies from place to place. The ancient Romans changed the word *karros* to *carrus*.

---

cau•tious•ly (kô´ shəs lē) *adverb*
In a careful way, without taking chances: *Children who walk to school should cross streets **cautiously**.*

clat•ter (klăt´ ər) *verb* To make a loud, rattling sound: *The baby sat on the kitchen floor and **clattered** the pots and pans.*

ă rat / ā pay / â care / ä father / ĕ pet / ē be / ĭ pit / ī pie / î fierce / ŏ pot / ō go / ô paw, for / oi oil /
ŏŏ took

coax (kōks) *verb* To try to persuade: *Gloria **coaxed** the cat to come down from the tree by offering it a bowl of milk.*

court (kôrt) *verb* To try to win the love of someone: *The young man sent red roses to the woman he wished to **court**.*

creak (krēk) *verb* To squeak: *Olga tried to tiptoe quietly down the stairs, but then one of the old floorboards **creaked**.*

D

dam•age (dăm´ ĭj) *noun* Harm: *Our new puppy did some **damage** to Dad's slipper when she chewed on it.*

damage

de•cent (dē´ sənt) *adjective* Proper: *It's not **decent** to borrow something from a friend and then not return it.*

de•fi•ant (dĭ fī´ ənt) *adjective* Showing a refusal to obey: *If you stamp your feet and shout "NO!" when told to do something, you are being **defiant**.*

dig•ni•fied (dĭg´ nə fīd´) *adjective* Acting in a proper or serious way: *The mayor is a **dignifed** woman, whom people of our town respect and look up to.*

dis•turb (dĭ stûrb´) *verb* To break in on or bother: *Do not **disturb** your sister while she is doing her homework.*

E

em•bank•ment (ĕm bāngk´ mənt) *noun* A small hill of dirt or rocks: *The **embankment** along the river keeps the water from flooding our fields during a storm.*

embankment

ōō b**oo**t / ou **ou**t / ŭ c**u**t / û f**u**r / hw **wh**ich / th **th**in / *th* **th**is / zh vi**s**ion / ə **a**bout, sil**e**nt, penc**i**l, lem**o**n, circ**u**s

em•bar•rassed (ĕm bār´ əst) *adjective* Feeling ill at ease: *Eli felt nervous or* **embarrassed** *when he saw that everyone else had brought a present to the party.*

en•gi•neer (ĕn´ jə nîr´) *noun* A person who runs the locomotive on a train: *When the* **engineer** *saw a deer on the tracks, he blew the whistle to scare the animal off.*

engineer

ENGINEER
This word was formed by adding the ending *-er,* meaning "one who," to the word *engine. Engine* comes from an Old French word meaning "skill."

glare (glâr) *verb* To look at someone in an angry way: *Mr. Brooks* **glared** *at Nan when he saw her taking a shortcut through his yard.*

glow•er (glou´ ər) *verb* To stare at in an angry or threatening way: *Mr. Brooks* **glowered** *at the kids who batted a baseball through his window.*

hail (hāl) *noun* Small pieces of frozen rain. Hail usually falls during a thunderstorm.

hail

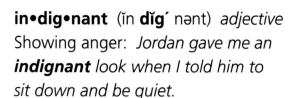

in•dig•nant (ĭn dĭg´ nənt) *adjective* Showing anger: *Jordan gave me an* **indignant** *look when I told him to sit down and be quiet.*

in•fec•tion (ĭn fĕk´ shən) *noun* A disease that can be passed from one person or animal to another: *The doctor gave Vanessa medicine to take for her throat* **infection.**

ă rat / ā pay / â care / ä father / ĕ pet / ē be / ĭ pit / ī pie / î fierce / ŏ pot / ō go / ô paw, for / oi oil / ōō took

in•sist (ĭn **sĭst´**) *verb* To demand: Grandpa **insisted** that Ari stop reading and go to sleep.

L

lo•cal (**lō´** kəl) *adjective* Making lots of stops: The **local** train takes longer than the express because it makes more stops.

LOCAL

Local comes from a Latin word meaning "place."

M

mend (mĕnd) *verb* To heal or get better: Mara's broken arm is **mending**, but it must remain in a cast for two more weeks.

mend

MEND

Mend is a shortened form of the word *amend,* which means "to change."

---

mod•est•ly (**mŏd´** ĭst lē) *adverb* In a humble way: Lynn bragged about winning the girls' race, but José accepted his first-place prize **modestly.**

N

no•ble•man (**nō´** bəl man) *noun* A man of high rank, often with a title: The king gave the **nobleman** land, money, and the title of duke.

nobleman

NOBLEMAN

Long ago, when people used the word *nobleman,* it meant "well-known man."

O

op•er•ate (**ŏp´** ə rāt´) *verb* To do surgery, as a doctor does: Dr. Brady **operated** on Bobby to take out his tonsils.

ōō b**oo**t / ou **ou**t / ŭ c**u**t / û f**u**r / hw **wh**ich / th **th**in / *th* **th**is / zh vi**s**ion / ə **a**bout, sil**e**nt, penc**i**l, lem**o**n, circ**u**s

329

P

pan•ic (**păn′** ĭk) *verb* To suddenly feel great fear: *When a wave washed Suki off her float, she started to panic.*

PANIC

The word *panic* comes from the name *Pan.* Pan was a god worshipped by the ancient Greeks. Pan caused fear in herds of cattle as well as in crowds of people.

---

pa•tient (**pā′** shənt) *noun* One being treated by a doctor or dentist: *Dr. Ramirez gave flu shots to many of her patients.*

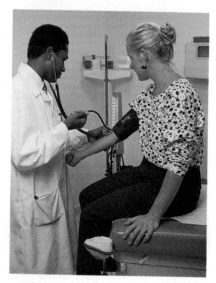

patient

PATIENT

Patient comes from a Latin word meaning "suffering."

---

plod (plŏd) *verb* To walk with great effort: *The snow was deep now, and people were plodding through it to get home.*

PLOD

Plod is a sound word. It imitates the sound someone makes as he or she walks with heavy footsteps.

---

pro•pos•al (prə **pō′** zəl) *noun* A plan or an offer: *Dad said, "I'll make you a proposal. If you clean your room, I'll take you to the movies."*

pro•test (**prō′** tĕst′) *verb* To complain: *Julio wanted to keep on swimming, so he protested when I said, "It's time to go home."*

R

re•lieved (rĭ **lĕvd′**) *adjective* Less worried: *I felt so relieved to see Rex that I didn't punish him for running off.*

re•luc•tant•ly (rĭ **lŭk′** tənt lē) *adverb* In a way that shows unwillingness: *Fran turned the TV off reluctantly because she didn't want to go to bed.*

ă rat / ā pay / â care / ä father / ĕ pet / ē be / ĭ pit / ī pie / î fierce / ŏ pot / ō go / ô paw, for / oi oil / o͝o took

rum•ble (**rŭm´** bəl) *noun* A deep, rolling sound, like distant thunder: *As we neared the amusement park, we could hear the **rumble** of the old roller coaster.*

S

sched•ule (**skĕj´** ōol) *or* (**skĕj´** əl) *noun* A list of the times when trains, buses, or planes arrive and depart: *Mike checked the **schedule** to see what time our train would arrive.*

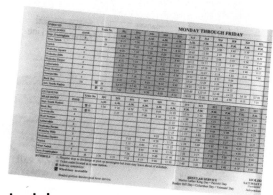

schedule

SCHEDULE

Schedule comes from the Latin word for "sheet of papyrus." Papyrus was what ancient Romans (and Egyptians) used for paper.

---

scoff (scŏf) *or* (scôf) *verb* To mock or laugh at: *Ted was surprised when Anna got a home run; he had **scoffed** at the idea of having a girl on the team.*

scowl (skoul) *verb* To frown angrily: *Jennifer **scowled** when she couldn't find her skates.*

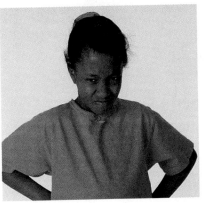

scowl

snick•er (snĭk´ ər) *verb* To laugh in a mean way: *Tony **snickered** when his dog jumped up and grabbed the hamburger I was about to eat.*

sol•emn (sōl´ əm) *adjective* Very serious: *To be on the team, you have to make a **solemn** promise to obey all the rules.*

spoil (spoil) *verb* **1.** To hurt someone's character by always giving in or by praising too much: *That little boy cries whenever he can't have what he wants; I think his family has **spoiled** him.* **2.** To ruin: *The rip **spoiled** Sam's new jacket.*

ōō bo**o**t / ou **ou**t / ŭ c**u**t / û f**u**r / hw **wh**ich / th **th**in / *th* **th**is / zh vi**s**ion / ə **a**bout, sil**e**nt, penc**i**l, lem**o**n, circ**u**s

sput•ter (**spŭt´** ər) *verb* To speak in a confused way; to stammer: *When we shouted "Happy birthday!" Helen was so surprised that she* **sputtered** *words no one could understand.*

strained (strānd) *adjective* Tense and uncomfortable: *Ken and I had had a fight, so our next phone conversation was* **strained.**

stride (strīd) *verb* To walk forward: *Gina* **strode** *up to the front of the classroom to give her report.*

sur•ger•y (**sûr´** jə rē) *noun* Operating on someone to remove or repair diseased body parts: *The doctor will need to perform* **surgery** *on Grandpa to repair his heart.*

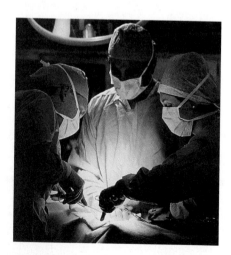

surgery

T

tem•per•a•ture (**tem´** pər ə chər) *noun* Hotness of one's body, as measured by a thermometer: *If your* **temperature** *is much above 98.6°F, you have a fever and may be sick.*

tor•na•do (tôr **nā´** dō) *noun* A violent kind of storm, in which winds spin around in a funnel-shaped cloud.

tornado

> ### TORNADO
> *Tornado* comes from the Spanish word *tronada*, which is a form of the verb *tronar*, meaning "to thunder."

ă rat / ā pay / â care / ä father / ĕ pet / ē be / ĭ pit / ī pie / î fierce / ŏ pot / ō go / ô paw, for / oi oil / ōō took

332

tri•um•phant•ly (trī **ŭm´** fənt lē) *adverb* In a way that shows happiness at having won or been successful: *After winning the football game, the team ran* **triumphantly** *from the field.*

TRIUMPHANTLY

This word comes from the Latin word *triumphus.* In ancient Rome, it referred to a parade honoring a general for victory over an enemy.

---

trudge (trŭj) *verb* To walk very slowly and with effort: *The children had to* **trudge** *through the deep snow to get to the bus stop.*

whine (wīn) *verb* To make a crying sound: *Whenever our dog wanted to go out, she sat at the front door and* **whined.**

whoop (ho͞op) *or* (hwo͞op) *or* (wo͞op) *verb* To cry out loudly: *When Scott got a home run, his team* **whooped** *with joy.*

wrecked (rĕkt) *adjective* Ruined: *I cried as I looked at my* **wrecked** *bike; I shouldn't have left it in the driveway.*

yield (yēld) *verb* To give in: *The horse wanted to run, but Betsy held the reins tightly and wouldn't* **yield***.*

---

o͞o b**oo**t / ou **ou**t / ŭ c**u**t / û f**u**r / hw **wh**ich / th **th**in / *th* **th**is / zh vi**si**on / ə **a**bout, sil**e**nt, penc**i**l, lem**o**n, circ**u**s

ACKNOWLEDGMENTS

For each of the selections listed below, grateful acknowledgment is made for permission to excerpt and/or reprint original or copyrighted material, as follows:

Selections

Brave Irene, written and illustrated by William Steig. Copyright © 1986 by William Steig. Reprinted by permission of Farrar, Straus & Giroux, Inc.

"A Calendar for Kids," from *The Second Kids' World Almanac of Records and Facts*, by Margo McLoone-Basta and Alice Siegel. Copyright © 1987 by Margo McLoone-Basta and Alice Siegel. Reprinted by permission of Funk & Wagnalls Corporation.

"Celebration," by Alonzo Lopez, from *Whispering Wind*, by Terry Allen. Copyright © 1972 by the Institute of American Indian Arts. Reprinted by permission of Doubleday, a division of Bantam Doubleday Dell Publishing Group, Inc. Illustration by Tomie dePaola, from *Tomie dePaola's Book of Poems*. Copyright © 1988 by Tomie dePaola. Reprinted by permission of G. P. Putnam's Sons.

Chicken Sunday, written and illustrated by Patricia Polacco. Copyright © 1992 by Patricia Polacco. Reprinted by permission of Philomel Books.

"Fun Food Facts," copyright © 1994 by Meredith Corporation. Reprinted by permission of *Crayola Kids*™ magazine. All rights reserved. Crayola® and Crayola Kids™ are trademarks of Binney & Smith Properties, Inc.

"Get the Facts on Fast Foods," from September 1993 *Current Health 1* magazine. Reprinted by permission of Weekly Reader Corporation.

"The Great Hair Argument," from *Ramona and Her Mother*, by Beverly Cleary. Copyright © 1979 by Beverly Cleary. Reprinted by permission of Morrow Junior Books, a division of William Morrow & Company, Inc.

"The Greatest Storms on Earth," from December 1992 *Kids Discover* magazine. Copyright © 1992 by Kids Discover Magazine. Reprinted by permission.

Halmoni and the Picnic, by Sook Nyul Choi, illustrated by Karen Milone Dugan. Text copyright © 1992 by Sook Nyul Choi. Illustrations copyright © 1992 by Karen Milone Dugan. Reprinted by permission of Houghton Mifflin Company. All rights reserved.

"How Snowmaker was taught a lesson," from *How we saw the world*, by C. J. Taylor. Copyright © 1993 by C. J. Taylor. Reprinted by permission of Tundra Books.

"I'd Never Eat a Beet," from *The New Kid on the Block*, by Jack Prelutsky. Copyright © 1984 by Jack Prelutsky. Reprinted by permission of William Morrow & Company.

Mac & Marie & the Train Toss Surprise, by Elizabeth Fitzgerald Howard, illustrations by Gail Gordon Carter. Text copyright © 1993 by Elizabeth Fitzgerald Howard. Illustrations copyright © 1993 by Gail Gordon Carter. Reprinted by permission of Simon & Schuster Books for Young Readers, Simon & Schuster Children's Publishing Division.

"Pronunciation Key," from the *American Heritage Children's Dictionary*. Copyright © 1994 by Houghton Mifflin Company. Reprinted by permission. All rights reserved.

"Ribsy and the Roast," from *Henry and Beezus*, by Beverly Cleary. Copyright © 1952 by Beverly Cleary. Reprinted by permission of William Morrow & Company, Inc.

"Sandwiches from Around the World," by Ann Hinga Klein. Copyright © 1994 by the Meredith Corporation. Reprinted by permission of *Crayola Kids*™ magazine. All rights reserved. Crayola® and Crayola Kids™ are trademarks of Binney & Smith Properties, Inc.

Say Woof! written and illustrated by Gail Gibbons. Copyright © 1992 by Gail Gibbons. Reprinted by permission of the author.

Storm in the Night, by Mary Stolz, illustrated by Pat Cummings. Text copyright © 1988 by Mary Stolz. Illustrations copyright © 1988 by Pat Cummings. Reprinted by permission of HarperCollins Publishers.

"This has been a good day!" from *As You Like It, Charlie Brown*, by Charles M. Schulz. Copyright © 1963, 64 by United Feature Syndicate, Inc. Reprinted by permission.

Tony's Bread, written and illustrated by Tomie dePaola. Copyright © 1989 by Tomie dePaola. Reprinted by permission of G. P. Putnam's Sons.

Tornado Alert, by Franklyn M. Branley. Copyright © 1988 by Franklyn M. Branley. Reprinted by permission of HarperCollins Publishers.

"Wind and Weather," from *175 Science Experiments to Amuse and Amaze Your Friends*, by Brenda Walpole, illustrated by Kuo Kang Chen and Peter Bull. Copyright © 1988 by Grisewood & Dempsey Ltd. Reprinted by permission of Random House, Inc.

Poetry

"Snowflakes," from *Half Past Four*, by Suk-Joong Yoon. Copyright © 1978 by Suk-Joong Yoon. Reprinted by permission of F. T. Yoon Company.

"Spaghetti! Spaghetti!" from *Rainy Rainy Saturday*, by Jack Prelutsky. Copyright © 1980 by Jack Prelutsky. Reprinted by permission of William Morrow & Company. Art from *Never Take a Pig to Lunch and Other Poems About the Fun of Eating*, by Nadine Bernard Westcott. Copyright © 1994 by Nadine Bernard Westcott. Reprinted by permission of Orchard Books.

"Sunflakes," from *Country Pie*, by Frank Asch. Copyright © 1979 by Frank Asch. Reprinted by permission of Greenwillow Books, a division of William Morrow & Company, Inc.

"That Kind Of Day," from *Under the Sunday Tree*, by Eloise Greenfield, paintings by Amos Ferguson. Text copyright © 1988 by Eloise Greenfield. Paintings copyright © 1988 by Amos Ferguson. Reprinted by permission of HarperCollins Publishers.

"Who Has Seen the Wind?" by Christina Rossetti, public domain.

Additional Acknowledgments

Special thanks to the following teachers whose students' compositions are included in this level:

Leticia Albright, E. A. Jones Elementary School, Missouri City, Texas; Alice Holstein, Dana Hall School, Newton, Massachusetts; Ron Gunter, Taylors Elementary School, Taylors, South Carolina; Theresa Callicott, North Jackson Elementary School, Jackson, Mississippi; Betsy Turner, Clays Mill Elementary School, Lexington, Kentucky; Jane Merritt, Mountainside Elementary School, Fort Carson, Colorado

CREDITS

Illustration 18–35 Tomie dePaola; 43–57 Karen M. Dugan; 62–81 Alan Tiegreen; 93–120 Patricia Polacco; 122–123 Greg Valley; 130–148 George Guzzi; 195–218 William Steig; 220, 222 C. J. Taylor; 232–253 Alan Tiegreen; 265–286 Gail Gordon Carter; 295–320 Gail Gibbons; 322 Tomie dePaola; 323 Charles M. Schulz

Photography 4-5 ©Naoki Okamoto/The Stock Market 6-7 J. Amos/H. Armstrong Roberts 36 Suki Coughlin(1994) 42 Courtesy of Sook Nyul Choi/Houghton Mifflin Co.(tl) 42 Courtesy of Karen Dugan(br) 82-83 Gary Cralle/The Image Bank 82 Courtesy of Beverly Cleary(t) 83 Lee Hunt 92 © 1994 Lawrence Migdale 93 © 1994 Lawrence Migdale 124-125 ©Jeffrey Brown/Liason International 130 Courtesy of Franklyn M. Branley(tl) 135 Barbara Van Cleve/Tony Stone Images(br) 142-143 Frank Rossotto/The Stock Market 148-149 ©Jeff Heger 1985/FPG International

150 ©Frank Rossotto/The Stock Market 150 ©Viviane Moos/The Stock Market 156-157 © 93 Wolf Maehl/ ZEFA/The Stock Market 187 Chip Porter/©Tony Stone Images 188 ©Rob Nelson/Courtesy of William Steig(bl) 188,189 ©Richard Pasley/Liason International 190 Merrilee Thomas 190 Kent Wood/Photo Researchers(m) 191 Sigrid Heilig/Photo Researchers 191 Howard Bluestein/Photo Researchers 191 The Granger Collection 192 D. Olsen/Weatherstock 192 Hasler & Pierce, NASA /GSFC/Science Photo Library 192-193 NOAA/ National Geophysical Data Center 193 Library of Congress 193 Brian Drake/Photo Researchers 193 Lawrence Migdale/Photo Researchers 224-225 Delauney, Robert Simultaneous Contrasts: Sun and Moon(1913; dated on painting 1912). Oil on canvas 53" diameter. The Museum of Modern Art, New York. Mrs. Simon Guggenheim Fund. Photograph (c) 1995 The Museum of Modern Art, New York. 254 Courtesy of Alan Tiegreen(b) 254 Courtesy of Beverly Cleary(t) 258 Obremski/The Image Bank(br) 258, 259 ©James Randkler/Tony Stone Images 259 David Jeffrey/The Image Bank(bm) 259 The Bettmann Archive(br) 259 Guido Rossi/The Image Bank(m) 260 Benn Mitchell/The Image Bank(tr) 260 The Bettmann Archive(ml) 260 G.V. Faint/The Image Bank(ml) 260 Ron Rovtar/FPG International(bm) 261 Jeff Hunter/The Image Bank(tl) 261 The Bettmann Archive(mr) 261 Kevin Forest/The Image Bank(bl) 261 Mel Digiacomo/The Image Bank(bm) 262 Co Rentmeester/The Image Bank(bl) 262 Micheal Quackenbush/The Image Bank(bm) 262 Michel Tcherevkoff/The Image Bank(m) 263 Phillip Kretchmar/The Image Bank(tl) 263 Richard Hutchings/Photo Researchers(tm) 263 UPI/Bettmann(bl) 286 Courtesy of Elizabeth Fitzgerald Howard(m) 286 Courtesy of Elizabeth Fitzgerald Howard(b) 288 Courtesy of Gail Gibbons(tm) 290 Courtesy of Jamie Coleman(br) 291 Rohan/ Tony Stone Images/Chicago Inc 291 Courtesy of Matthew Uckotter(tr) 292 Max Gibbs/Animals Animals 292 Courtesy of Beverly Hernandez(tl) 293 W. Anthony/West Stock 293 Courtesy of Joe Sturdivant(tr)